W. Lee-Warner

Citizen of India

W. Lee-Warner

Citizen of India

ISBN/EAN: 9783337385613

Printed in Europe, USA, Canada, Australia, Japan

Cover: Foto ©Suzi / pixelio.de

More available books at **www.hansebooks.com**

THE
CITIZEN OF INDIA

BY

W. LEE-WARNER, C.S.I., M.A.

FELLOW OF THE UNIVERSITY OF BOMBAY, AND FORMERLY ACTING DIRECTOR OF PUBLIC INSTRUCTION IN BERAR AND BOMBAY, AND MEMBER OF THE EDUCATION COMMISSION, 1882-83

Macmillan and Co., Limited

London, Bombay, and Calcutta

1897

PREFACE.

THE world has grown wiser and older by a century and a half since a famous French poet and philosopher offered the advice that a nation should cultivate its garden and rest content with that object in life. In the East as well as in the West men have now a wider outlook. They begin to take an interest, and consequently a part, in carrying on and even shaping their governments. From the West, which owes so much in the past to the Aryan race, India has in turn received freedom, free speech, free trade, free movement. The mass of the population remains uneducated, and cannot tell whence comes the new spirit that moves on the face of the waters. But the spirit blows, and all men hear the sound thereof, and are stirred by its breath. The education of those who pass through our schools does not end in the school-room, and for those who are classed as "unable to read or write" it begins in the village, in the municipal town, in the courts of law, and on the railways. Knowledge or ignorance, truth or error, must circulate like the currency through the multitudes. It cannot be a matter of indifference what lessons we teach to the young, for what they learn they will pass on to others. Whether they are trained in the right path, or left to stray into prejudice, intolerance, and disloyalty to their neighbours, the rising generation are born to be citizens. An effort ought to be made to teach our future citizens the A B C of their rights and duties. Who am I, and who are my neighbours? How am I governed and what is expected of me? What becomes of the taxes I pay? What is done to keep me and my property safe, and to protect me from disease and famine? These are questions which must occur to many, and they lead up to the further question: What is my duty to my neighbour? It is the main purpose of the author of this little volume to place before Indian school-boys a few simple facts about the land in which they live; but it is believed that older citizens of the British Empire may find in its pages some information about India which will be of interest to them. Be that as it may, the author at least ventures to hope that his work may lead some of the rising generation in India to value their heritage of British citizenship, and to acknowledge the duties which they owe to themselves and their fellow countrymen.

W. L.-W.

November 5, 1897.

CONTENTS.

CHAPTER IV.

CHAPTER V.

CHAPTER VI.

CHAPTER VII.

CHAPTER VIII.

CHAPTER IX.

CHAPTER X.

CHAPTER XI.

CHAPTER XII.

LIST OF ILLUSTRATIONS.

CHAPTER I.

THE VILLAGE.

1. **Common Interests.** Every schoolboy in India who has made such progress in his studies as to be able to read this book will be in a position to understand the two following simple statements. The first is, that the ties which ought to unite men as citizens of one and the same country need not be broken, or even strained, by the mere fact that they profess different religious creeds, or adopt different modes of life. The second is, that the unity of a society composed of various classes can best be promoted by enlarging their knowledge and the sympathy of each class with its neighbours, and by studying their privileges and duties as citizens of a common country. Men who live together in the same land must constantly work for, and with, each other. They have in fact common interests, and if any one should ask what is meant by common interests, he cannot do better than think of his own body. Nearly four hundred years before the beginning of the Christian era a wise man of Greece explained the subject in these terms. "The best ordered state," said Socrates, "is that in which the

greatest number of men use the expressions—'this is mine' or 'this is not mine'—in the same way and in reference to the same object." He went on to illustrate his argument by the following example—"If only the finger of a man is hurt, then the whole frame, drawn towards the soul as a centre and forming a united kingdom under one ruler, feels the hurt and sympathizes with it; and we all say that the man has a pain in his finger." The man with all his members takes the part, and feels the hurt, of any member affected. That which is true of a single man is true also of a community of men living in one country under one ruler, or, as it is often called, the "body politic." If one village suffers, the province should feel the pain in its village; or if the province suffers, the country should suffer with it. The interests of one class are the interests of all, and the best ordered empire is that in which the greatest number of citizens sympathize with each other.

2. **Elements of Union in India.** Just as the members of the body perform different duties, and are in form and other respects unlike each other, although they all minister to the common safety and well-being of the body, so a living unity of heart and mind in a great population can exist side by side with differences of creed and habits. In European countries there is a very keen sense of personal liberty and of freedom of conscience, which tends to draw not merely large classes, but also families and individuals, apart from their near neighbours. The tendency to separation is, however, corrected by a national respect for law and a general feeling of patriotism. In India these binding influences of law and love of country were not in

former days cultivated. But, on the other hand, the inhabitants have from time immemorial possessed certain traits of character and customs, conducive to union, which western countries have lacked. Personal devotion to a chief, obedience to the father of a family, a strong sense of religion, and village communities have in the past laid in India a foundation for useful citizenship. The people have long since felt in the family circle, in the religious sect, or in village life, the practical advantages of common action. To a large extent men have been accustomed to look beyond themselves, and to feel that they are members of a wider circle than that of their own separate families. The village and the caste system have thus introduced into the daily life of the country an idea of co-operation, and a feeling that, if one caste of labourers supplies one want of the village or the nation, its wants should be supplied in turn by other castes. The spirit of mutual helpfulness, and the sense, shared by all classes, of dependence upon government and a higher providence, are influences which even to-day tend to draw the people of India towards each other. On the other hand, the very system of family, caste, and creed which has fostered them, is sometimes apt to restrict the operation of these influences to a narrow circle. The natives of India are famed for their charity, but their charity is more confined within the caste or the sect than is the case in Europe. The citizen ought to have a wider range of duties and privileges than any class or sect of the community can have. As the family is merged in the village, so the village is merged in the province, and the province in the empire, and by citizenship we mean membership of the whole Indian empire, with the rights and obligations which such membership implies. In order that each citizen may know what he owes to his fellow countrymen and to his government, he has to some extent to shake himself free of prejudices, and to remember that, besides his duty to his family or sect or village, he owes something to the whole country of which he has inherited the right to call himself a citizen.

3. **The Village Community.** The current of the people's life in a healthy state of society ought to flow through the family and the village into the province, and so forth to the whole empire. In times past each Indian village was a separate, and rather stagnant, centre of national life. The village community contained in miniature all the materials of the State. Within its walls or ring-fences families of different castes or religions dwelt together, supplying each other's daily wants, and uniting to defend their homes when attacked by an enemy, who generally came from a neighbouring village or province. All that the inhabitants knew of government and of the duties of the State to its subjects was collected before their eyes. Public authority was represented by the head-man, who united in himself the several functions of collector of revenue, of police superintendent, of magistrate, and even of civil judge. He was aided by an assistant, and by the village accountant. The other officials who took part in the public administration were the silversmith who assayed money, and the village watchman who tracked thieves, carried messages, guarded the boundaries, and arrested wrongdoers.

Outside these official classes were other families

which ministered to the wants of the community, bound to their neighbours by the ties of common interests, and rendering to them services in return for a share of the village produce and the protection which they received. They were the village blacksmith, the carpenter, the potter, the grass-rope maker, the sweeper, the cobbler, the barber, the washerman, and the water-carrier. The expenses of carrying on the affairs of the village and of managing the temple were met by a tax upon the lands or the houses of the village. Such is the picture of a little State contained in the village, which was drawn by a writer who was well acquainted with native society in the Dekhan in the year 1820.

4. The Past and the Present. The striking changes which India has witnessed in the last century have greatly changed the people's mode of life. The appearance of the villages themselves has altered: the rules which compelled the inhabitants to remain attached to their villages have been repealed, and the large powers which were concentrated in the hands of the village officers have been divided. If you should look at a picture of any good-sized village as it appeared in 1820 you would see that it was walled round, or at least defended by a stout fence of prickly pear. In some of the native states, and in all the countries bordering on India, the villages are to-day in a similar state of defence, as if they expected attacks at night. Their walls and fences, no doubt, offer a substantial obstacle to the intrusion of robbers, but they also oppose the passage of free air, and otherwise interfere with ventilation and sanitary habits. It was in the interests of public health that the fine old walls of

THE PALACE GATE, DELHI.

Ahmedabad were partially demolished, but the gates are for the most part still preserved.

The interior arrangements of the village used to correspond to its exterior. The artizans could not leave their homes without great difficulty. At home their services were at the disposal of the government for the performance of forced labour, or else at the call of the villagers in return for certain moderate dues or shares of the village-produce fixed by custom with a sparing hand. In any case it was not convenient to let them emigrate until famine left them without their shares of grain. Then again the village officers exercised very large authority over the rest of the inhabitants. In short, all that the village thought about was itself and its lands, and all that it knew about justice and government was contained in the authority of its head-man. It was walled off from the rest of the country in more senses than one. To-day the village walls are thrown down, and its prickly pear is severely pruned. The postman brings its newspapers from the capital of the province, and the villagers may go where they like in search of employment and profit. The divisional and district courts outside its limits are open to receive any complaints which the humblest inhabitant may prefer.

5. **The Merits of the Old System.** A statesman, Mountstuart Elphinstone, whose name is still connected with the leading college and high school of Bombay, and who felt a high admiration for the virtues of Indian rural society, expressed the opinion that the village communities were probably "not suited to a good form of government." But he added, "they are

an excellent remedy for the imperfections of a bad one, and they prevent the bad effects of its negligence and weakness, and even present some barriers against its tyranny." Every one must admit that there was much that was attractive in the picture of village society which has just been drawn. The villagers were taught to render services to each other, to work for each other according to their several trades, to depend upon each other, and to stand shoulder to shoulder in self-defence. At a time when disorder reigned, and the rulers employed no police to protect their subjects, the people were enabled to provide to some extent for their own safety. If the higher revenue officials exacted from the raiyats more than they could pay, the village rose up as one man to resist the demand. If families quarrelled, the public opinion of the village restrained them, and although the head-men combined executive with judicial powers, they had sometimes the united pressure of their fellow-villagers to correct them in the discharge of their duties. The provinces frequently changed hands and passed from one native ruler to another, but the village life usually ran on in an even course or without much alteration. The villagers sowed and reaped, even though their rulers carried off as much of the crop as they could.

6. **Faults of the Old System.** There was, however, another side to the picture which was not so pleasant. The villages received no real protection from government, and no help in time of distress. Their inhabitants had no motives of self-interest, no spirit of competition, to stimulate their labour or induce them to improve their condition. It will be well to realize the condition of Indian villages in past times in these

several respects, and the consequences which flowed from them. It is the duty of a government to protect its subjects from foreign foe and civil disorder. But a government can only do this effectively if it can call to its aid the united resources of the whole country. The independent action of a number of isolated villages is of no use in repelling a strong enemy. India learnt this to her cost when a Tamerlane, or a Nadir Shah, laid her capital cities in the dust, deluging their streets with blood. As foreign armies marched upon Delhi or any other city they over-ran the villages in their path, destroying crops and property, and converting the tilled land into a desert. The forces of the native rulers did their best to defend the capital towns, but they left the villages to their fate. Even in times of peace the public taxes were spent on the adornment of the cities—Delhi, Agra, Fatehpur Sikri, Bijapur, and others—whilst nothing was spent on district canals and roads or public works of local benefit. At times also it was not even a foreign foe, but an unruly band of Pindaris or organized plunderers living in India, who inflicted misery on the villages. The fate of Guntur which perished with all its families in the flames lit by its own inhabitants, in order to escape the hands of the Pindaris, was not unknown to other villages in the Dekhan. In times of famine or pestilence the State took no action to save the lives and properties of the suffering masses. In short, the governments in former days left the villages without any attempt to rescue or assist them, and the consequence was that the word patriotism, or love of country, was unknown in India. If the rulers of the country did not treat their subjects as children, it was only natural that the people should confine their regard to their village magnates and local leaders, and entertain no feeling of love or devotion for their country at large.

Within the village itself there was no motive for industry or improvement. The cultivators saw their crops removed and a bare subsistence left to them, no matter what care or industry they bestowed upon their fields. The artizans worked without reward for the State, or else for each other in return for a small customary payment in kind. The traders were often obliged to sell their goods at a fixed price, and their operations could not extend to distant places when the country was full of disorder and the roads insecure.

But with all these drawbacks the villagers held together, and bent their heads before the storms which blew over them. By the ties of family feeling and common defence village society was kept united, isolated it is true, but still able to rise up again after numerous falls and disasters. If the villagers lived always in a state of siege, at least they lived, and the village sites survived the revolutions which overtook the province. Their nominal rulers changed constantly, but village life, hard at all times, suffered no very great change, whatever might befall the country or the province. In short, the poorest occupant of a hut in an Indian village may boast that he still occupies the site in the palm grove which his forefathers selected many centuries ago.

7. **The Modern Village.** The Indian village has ceased to be a state in miniature enclosed within walls and fences. It is an integral part of the province and so of the empire. Its barriers are broken down, and

INDIAN VILLAGE

the eyes of its inhabitants are fixed upon the outside world, in full confidence that their attention will not be required every night upon the walls of their village defences. All are free to go where self-interest leads them, and the hand of government is visible wherever they go. The raiyats know exactly what assessment they have to pay, and the profits of extra diligence and care go into their own pockets. There is no wasteful dispute about the share of the standing crops belonging to the state, and there is no need to bribe the official gatherer of their rents. Every cultivator or proprietor knows precisely what will be demanded of him, and the State takes no more than the sum which is entered in the public accounts. The classes owning no land of their own who live by labour, and the artizans of the village, can go where they please in search of employment, and many of them find work for a few months in the great cities, returning home for the rainy season. The village traders supply the merchants who keep their eyes fixed on the world's markets, and they sell the village crops where they can obtain the best prices. The protection of government is felt in every direction by every class, and instead of mud huts the people live in houses of brick and stone. The villagers are neither attacked at home by robbers in the night, nor are their houses laid in ruins by an invading army. When they go forth on their business they travel safely by roads or railways connecting their homes with distant cities. Even the village well is frequently not the sole supply of water. Each village shares with others the benefits of the canals which traverse the country, and the links which unite the villages with the large towns of the province are numerous. The authority of the village officers is regulated by law, and the civil and criminal courts held at headquarters are open to all. The village school leads on to the subdivisional school, and that to the district high school. Even the village registrar collects his returns of births and deaths, and regularly sends them on to a central office. Thus every one of the 537,901 villages and towns, in which 221 millions of people live in British India, maintains its identity as a distinct village, but feels at the same time that it is only a living part of the great empire to which it belongs.

8. **A Matter of Experience.** When once it is understood that the interests of every village are bound up with those of others, every one who can read or write must wish to learn something about the working of the great machine which carries on the public administration. He knows from his own experience that his village belongs to a district, and the district to a province, and he ought to have some idea as to how the provinces were formed, and what are their relations to the empire at large. When he goes out into the country he will probably cross the boundary of a native state, and he will find that he has stepped outside the jurisdiction of British courts. He has to live by the side of people of different creeds and races, and he will take more interest in them if he knows how their ancestors found their way into India, and what qualities they have brought to the common stock of the country. Other questions will be constantly suggested by matters within his daily observation. Whence comes the machinery which is opening the mines under the earth, or driving cotton mills in the

cities? How is the peace maintained in so vast a country, and how is the public health preserved? The practical experience of every man will give rise to these and other similar questions, and if education is of any value it ought to assist him in giving correct answers to them.

9. Personal Duty. For the answer is not a matter in which we have no concern. Its character for good or evil depends to a large extent upon our own efforts. The human body cannot enjoy health if the several members do not work together for it. In the same way the government of a country cannot be carried on if the citizens do not take an active part in assisting it. It is not at all necessary that a man should be in the service of the State in order to fulfil his duty to the State. We hear sometimes complaints of the corruption of the police, of the miscarriage of justice, or of the spread of disease which can be prevented. But bribes would not be taken if they were not offered, false evidence must be given before justice is perverted, and disease would not spread if it were not first produced and diffused by neglect of proper precautions. The country has a right to expect that each citizen will use his best endeavours to promote the causes of justice and public health. Within the village community there used to be a spirit of mutual help and service for the common good. Although the sphere of our duties is enlarged, there is no reason why the same idea should not animate the residents of a province or a country. In an address delivered in Calcutta in December, 1896, the Honourable Mr. Justice Ranade, C.I.E., made these observations: "The State after all exists only to make individual members composing it nobler, happier, richer, and more perfect in every attribute with which we are endowed: and this perfection of our being can never be insured by any outside arrangement, however excellent, unless the individual member concerned is in himself prepared in his own private social sphere of duties to co-operate in his own well-being."

10. **The Future.** If Mr. Ranade's excellent advice were more generally followed, we might look forward to the future as described by an English poet, Lewis Morris,

"There shall come from out the noise of strife and groaning,
  A broader day, a juster brotherhood·
A deep equality of aim postponing
  All selfish seeking to the general good.
There shall come a time when each shall to the other
Be as God would have him, brother to brother."

CHAPTER II.

THE CITY.

11. **Towns.** Before we proceed from the village to the district, we must learn something about the town or city. The population of the villages is called rural, and that of the towns urban. There are two points which should be noticed in dealing with the urban population of India. The first is that it is extremely small, as compared with what we find in England and in most other European countries. The other is, that it has greatly increased under British rule. In England and Wales, which cover only 58,309 square miles with about 29 millions of people, there are 185 towns, each containing more than 20,000 inhabitants, and all together counting an urban population of 15½ millions. In the whole of India, including the native states, with its huge area of 1,560,160 square miles, there are 225 such towns, of which only 38 are in the native states. The population of these 225 towns was returned in 1891 at less than 14 millions. It may be said that in one portion of the British Isles more than half the population lives in towns severally containing more than 20,000 inhabitants, while in

India not even a twentieth part resides in such towns. At the same time the urban population of British India has grown considerably in the last fifty years, and it is very much denser than in the native states.

12. **Advantages of Towns.** If any one should feel surprise at the small number of Indian towns, he will find an explanation of the fact in the state of the country before the arrival of the British. Three influences induce men to draw away from the villages and live together in large towns, namely, self-defence, trade, and the privileges of self-government which are generally granted to large towns and cities. One might have expected that in the centuries of invasion and civil war through which India has passed the people would have preferred towns to villages as affording to them a better protection. But the terrible fate which overtook Delhi and other cities warned the people that their frequent invaders, whose object was plunder and not government, would assuredly attack the wealthy city and not the poor village. Large towns attracted not merely the foreign foe, but also the cupidity of their rulers, and they were even liable to be moved from one place to another to please the whim or ambition of a prince. The ruins of many cities of Delhi bear witness to this experience. The influence of self-defence, which has proved elsewhere so strong in the formation of town colonies, was greatly weakened in India by these considerations.

Trade could never flourish in India when the country was exposed to internal disorder and foreign invasion. The population barely sufficed to keep the villages populated and their lands tilled; and although there were cities whose industries in copperware, silk fabrics, muslins, and lacquer work, obtained for them a reputation not confined to India, there was neither a large demand for these products of industry in the country, nor any safe means of exporting them to foreign countries. At present if the urban population of England shows signs of decrease, the inference is at once drawn that the foreign trade of Great Britain is falling off; but the trade which India carried on with other countries up to the establishment of British rule was a commerce in the produce of the land and the forests, and not in the products of skilled labour. India sent abroad her pepper, lac, fibres, ginger, and timber, and her trade stimulated the rural rather than the urban population. The value of Dacca [1] muslins exported in 1787 was thirty lakhs, but in 1813 it had fallen to less than four lakhs.

The third influence which leads men from the countryside to the town was unknown to India before British rule. Such small measure of self-government as the people enjoyed was confined to the village whose institutions were described in the last chapter. Even in the present day the progress of municipal life is slow, and such must be the case until the class of residents who possess wealth, education, and leisure is largely increased. In the meanwhile, as the towns increase under the influences of peace and trade, every opportunity is taken to entrust to the townsmen powers of self-government.

13. **Municipal Towns.** It is then to these towns that attention must be paid by those who wish to learn

[1] The muslins of Dacca were famous in Roman and even Assyrian times.

something about the machine of government. Leaving on one side for the present the three capital cities of Calcutta, Madras, and Bombay, and Rangoon the chief

THE EARL OF MAYO, K.P., 1869 TO 1872.

town of British Burma, we find that British India possessed in 1896 no less than 733 municipalities of which the population numbered 13,298,613 persons.

Bombay had 170 of them, the Punjab 149, Bengal 146, and the North Western Provinces 103. In Madras there were 56 such towns, and in the Central Provinces 53, the remainder being distributed in small numbers over the rest of India.

14. **Self-government.** The objects which the British authorities have kept in view in creating municipal boards in India have been two-fold—first, to enlist local interest in the management of local funds devoted to education, sanitation, medical charity, and local public works, and, secondly, to serve as instruments of political education. The former view was insisted upon by Lord Mayo in 1870 in a Resolution dated the 11th of February, and the second was enlarged upon by Lord Ripon in 1881-1882. It has been the steady purpose of Lord Ripon's successors to unite both policies. Before the government of India passed to the Crown in 1857, the East India Company had already conferred municipal powers upon the larger cities, and also in Bombay, upon several towns as far back as 1850. But no general advance was made throughout the country until the years 1871-1873, when several Acts were passed which were amended and enlarged in 1883 and 1884. Prior to 1883 there was a tendency to keep municipalities in leading strings, and to subject them to constant official control. The intention was to see that their powers were not ill-used, and their revenues not misapplied. After that year it was recognized that by removing official control in some cases, and in other cases by legally defining the limits of the State's interference, the people might be brought to take increased interest in local affairs, and so learn to devote to them the same care and

attention that they bestow upon their own concerns. The expression self-government indicates that within certain defined limits the authorities entrust to non-official bodies of citizens various powers of administration, which otherwise would be exercised by the officers of government.

15. **Trustees for the Public.** In order that self-government may not be discredited by neglect or other scandals, the State in delegating to these bodies or boards some of its own authority and powers, expressly reserves to itself a right to compel municipalities to exercise their lawful powers in cases of dangerous epidemics or other grave public necessity. It also defines precisely the class of taxes which the boards may levy, and the objects to which their funds are to be applied. The total revenue raised by the 733 municipalities in the year 1895 was about 249 lakhs, and this large income was spent by the people themselves on their own local wants through their trustees, the municipal committees or boards. Two instances may be given to explain the nature and objects of the restrictions imposed by the State on the powers of boards to raise taxes. In India the form of tax which is least felt, because it is least observed, is a tax upon articles of consumption called octroi. It is only fair that the residents of municipalities, numbering 13,298,613 persons, should tax themselves to supply local wants, but it is not fair that other consumers, who do not live in municipal limits, should be taxed for objects of no interest to them. Some years ago the richest municipality in Sindh was a mere village on the Indus where corn was brought to be carried down the river to a foreign market. The levy of octroi upon this

corn taxed not the municipal residents but the distant consumers of the corn, and thus it tended to drive Indian corn out of the market by raising its price. To prevent such practices an estimate is made of the extreme limit of the corn or other article which the population of the town can possibly consume, and if the municipal tax levied on that article produces a revenue much in excess of what such a tax upon the local consumption would give, a case arises for the interference of government. Another instance of restriction is afforded by the rule that the general taxation of the empire must not be injured by municipal finance. If the State raises a revenue from certain articles, the town must not tax those articles; otherwise it might destroy the trade in them, and so injure the public revenues.

As regards expenditure, municipal boards must not be extravagant with the monies entrusted to them by the State for a special object. The needs for which they are expected to provide are the conservancy and cleanliness of the town, its public health and dispensaries, its water-supply, roads, and other local public works, and primary education. It is the duty of the State, to whom the residents of the towns pay general taxes in addition to those levied by the municipality, to provide for the public peace, justice, military charges, the district police, and the cost of all general establishments in which the municipal residents are interested as subjects of the State.

16. **Political Education.** The general principle just stated can easily be understood. Within the town the inhabitants require many special conveniences of lighting, water, drainage, and medical comforts, which they

can thoroughly appreciate. For these local advantages they tax themselves, and the State entrusts to their representatives the duty of applying the local income to local wants. Within the municipal area the commissioners, some of whom are elected by the people themselves, carry on the local government under the legal powers conferred upon them by the State. This is what is called local self-government, and its success depends not merely on the ability of the members of the boards, but also upon the influence of local public opinion. If the citizens unite to oppose abuses of authority and suggest improvements, their views are sure to carry the day. This is what Lord Ripon meant by the phrase, "instruments of political education." The municipal commissioners are taught by experience to administer a public trust, and the citizens learn for themselves many lessons which they might be tempted to forget without it. The municipal residents find out by degrees that their votes and opinions may become a force which acts upon the local authorities. Each citizen can thus feel that he is a part of the government of his own town. He is raised to a new sense of right and duty, and the prosperity of the town becomes a source of pride to its whole population.

17. **Calcutta.** The rise of Calcutta from a mere collection of huts in 1700, when the village was bought by the English from a son of the Emperor Aurangzeb, to its present position as a city of palaces and the capital of India, illustrates the action of the three forces—protection, trade, and municipal honours—to which attention has been called. Its present prosperity is entirely due to the maintenance of the public peace, and to the triumph of science over natural obstacles.

The Company's first care was to free the settlement from the attacks of the Marathas, whose bands had penetrated Bengal from the western side of India. In 1756 the fort was captured by Suraj-ad-Daula, and after the tragedy of the "black hole," the British occupation and the very name of Calcutta were for a short time wiped out. But the successes of Clive in recapturing the city, and then in winning the decisive victory of Plassey on June 23, 1757, gave a fresh start to Calcutta, and in 1773 it was recognized as the capital of British India. Since that year its progress has never been interrupted by any serious local disturbance.

Calcutta, far more than Bombay, owes its favourable position as a trade-centre to the triumph of human skill and science over natural obstacles. In 1853 serious alarm was felt at the constant silting up of the Hughli's channel by which ocean steamers carry the commerce of Bengal to the sea, distant some 80 miles. It seemed as if Calcutta might follow the fate of Thana in the western presidency, but ceaseless observations, skilled pilotage, and gigantic dredgers have repaired the mischiefs caused by currents, and although the anchorage is at times visited by cyclones, yet the city holds its own as the first port of British India, the value of its trade in 1895-96 having been 72 crores of rupees. The river side is crowded with jetties and warehouses, and the population has risen by leaps and bounds from a few fishermen to 180,000 in 1822, to 361,370 in 1850, and now to more than 800,000 persons.

Municipal honours have added to its growth and lustre. Its affairs are conducted by 50 commissioners, of whom 25 are elected by their fellow-citizens, 10 are chosen by public bodies, and 15 nominated by government. The office of commissioner is one of dignity, and it becomes a stepping stone to higher positions. The annual income at the command of the commissioners is about 45 lakhs, and they have incurred debt to the extent of 238 lakhs.

18. **Bombay**. The city of Bombay, second in respect of trade to the capital of India, is the first of all the cities of India in population and wealth. It has never during the British occupation known the reverses which have overtaken Calcutta and Madras, although its protection from its near neighbours the Marathas, and from the pirates whom neither Hindu nor Mahomedan rulers of India could effectively control, has required constant care and effort. When the British crown received the place as part of the dowry of Catherine Braganza, Queen of Charles II., its revenues were calculated at 51,542 Rs. a year, and its population at "10,000 fugitives and vagabonds." In 1716 its population was only 16,000, and in 1816 it was 161,550. But in 1872 it had risen to 644,405, and in the last census it was 821,764. Its growth from a collection of fishermen's huts, lying on sandy waste and unwholesome swamp, to the present stately city of splendid buildings and beautiful gardens is almost marvellous. When the British first occupied it, the air was so pestilential that seven governors died in the space of thirty years, and no European children could survive a residence in it. Liable as it still is to serious outbreaks of disease and plague, it is on the whole healthy. In natural scenery few cities in the world can compete with it. The whole secret

of this wonderful change is to be found in British protection. The ships which visited the western coast of India in times past were afraid to anchor in the splendid harbour of Bombay. They therefore sought refuge up the stream behind the little forts in the Thana creek or at Kalyan. Even long after the dockyard was made at Bombay in 1671, the harbour continued to be infested with pirates, whose refuges and forts were not destroyed until 1756. The Marathas threatened the settlement for some years later, until the victory won at Kirkee in 1817 led to the establishment of peace and the creation of the Presidency of Bombay. Other difficulties in course of time interfered with the prosperity of the settlement, which, being situated on an island, had little room to expand. The waters of the sea were, however, excluded from the flats by the construction of the Vellard in 1771. By these means Bombay, protected at last by sea and land, advanced rapidly in population and trade. Fugitives from the dreaded inquisition at Goa found a refuge there, and during the disturbances which devastated the Dekhan and Guzerat, when the Maratha chiefs were struggling for supremacy, a continuous stream of settlers sought protection under the British flag. The Duke of Wellington described the city in April, 1804, as a general asylum for the oppressed. "This island," he wrote, "has now become the only place of security in this part of India for property, and for those who are objects of the Peshwa's enmity and vengeance, thus affording the strongest proof of the confidence which the natives repose in the justice and wisdom of our policy and our laws." Indeed, the popularity of the British courts of law led to

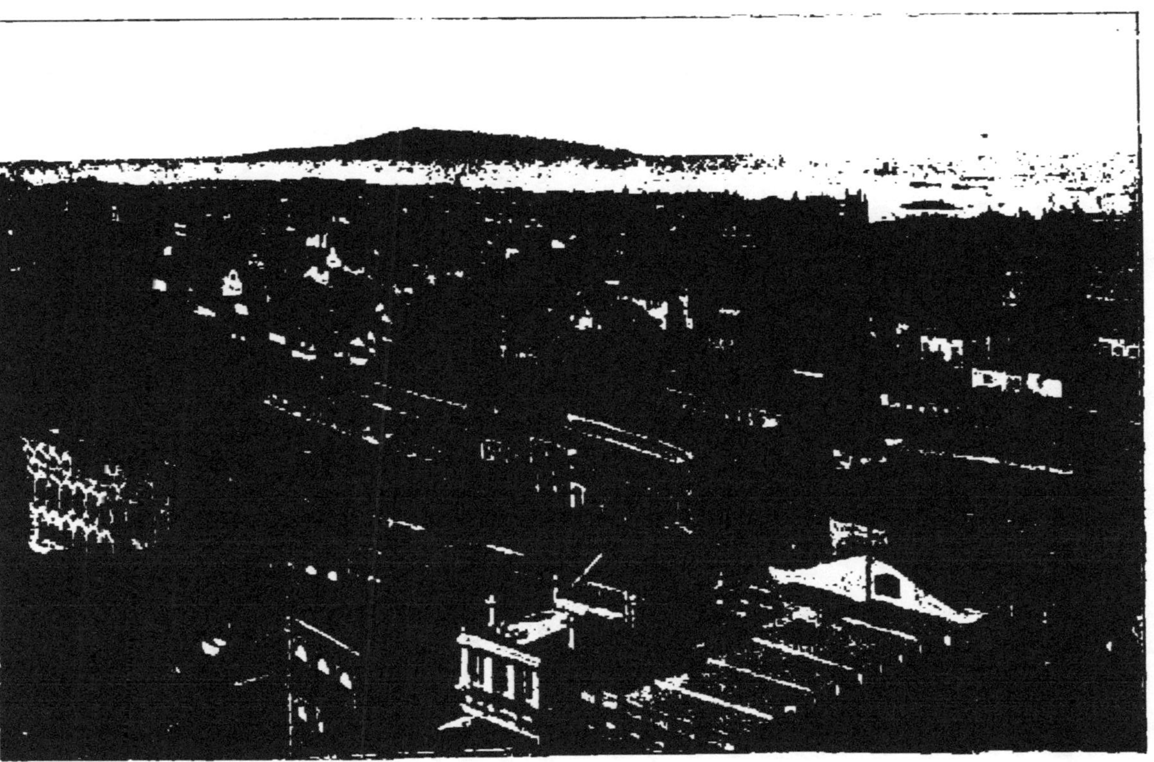

BOMBAY FROM THE TOP OF THE CLOCK TOWER.

such an increase of expenditure that the Company con plained. The Mayor's Court, the Court of Request and the Recorder's Court could not cope with th work, and at length, in the reign of George IV., th Supreme Court was established, and its jurisdictio extends even to remote Zanzibar and Aden.

That trade should follow in the wake of protectio was a matter of course in the case of a harbour situate like Bombay, and defended by the naval power c England. In 1802 the annual trade of the port together with that of Surat, was worth less than crore and a half. In 1895-96 it was worth nearl 66 crores of rupees At the end of the eighteentl century cotton was being exported to China, but nov the people of India have been taught to work up thei own cotton, and to export to China cotton goods. Th first cotton mill of the Bombay cotton spinning an weaving company was erected in 1854, and there ar now in the city and Presidency of Bombay 101 spinnin and weaving mills. Of factories of all sorts there ar 124 in the city alone, employing nearly 100,000 workmen.

It is impossible to contemplate the trade and the population of Bombay without a sense both of pride and duty. The municipal government of the city is entrusted to a corporation of 71 members, of whom 36 are chosen by the ratepayers, 15 by government, and the rest by various public bodies. The chief sects of the citizens are represented in it—the Parsis by 24 members, the Europeans by 17, the Hindus by 16, the Mahomedans by 12, and the Portuguese by 2 commissioners. The annual revenue at their disposal is about 67 lakhs of rupees, and the administration of this revenue as a public trust for the welfare of so large a population cannot fail to be a powerful factor in the political education of the people. The splendour of the municipal office is sufficient of itself to indicate the dignity and importance of self-government in Bombay.

19. **Madras.** The city of Madras has sprung from even a smaller origin than Bombay, but it possesses none of the advantages for trade which either the Hughli or the western harbour enjoys. The site on which it stands was granted to the Company by a raja in 1639, and the town and fort built upon it were exposed to attack both by sea and land. In 1741 the Marathas attacked the fort, and five years later the French captured it. After its restoration to the English, it was again besieged by the French in 1758, but since that siege it has enjoyed the blessings of peace. Unfortunately the roadstead is sometimes swept by hurricanes, and engineering skill can never do for Madras what it has done for Calcutta. The extension of railways and the construction of the Buckingham Canal have done much to counteract the natural disadvantages of the site of the city, and its trade, population, and revenues have increased under British protection. In 1871 the population was 397,552, and the municipal income about 5½ lakhs. Its population is now 452,518, and its municipal revenue about 13 lakhs a year. The value of its trade is about 11 crores of rupees. The affairs of the city are administered by a president and 40 members, of whom 30 are elected.

20. **Rangoon.** The history of this promising city is quite modern. Taken in 1824 during the first

VIEW OF MADRAS FROM THE PIER.

Burmese war, Rangoon was restored after the war, and soon after its recapture in 1852 it was injured by fire. Fortunate in the possession of a navigable river, it was made a city in 1880, and its foreign trade, now valued at 12 crores of rupees, already exceeds the trade of Madras. Its population numbers 180,324, and their affairs are administered by a committee of 24, of whom 18 are elected. Of the members 22 are non-officials, and 8 are natives. The municipal income is about 21 lakhs a year, and there is every prospect that this capital of the province of British Burma will eclipse Mandalay, at present a more populous town, not merely in the growth of trade, but also in its population.

21. **Capital Cities.** The four cities just described are the great trading centres of India, and exhibit in its most impressive form the working of self-government. But there are other cities in India which deserve a passing notice. Karachi, with a population of 105,199, already carries on a trade almost as valuable as that of Madras. Lahore, with a population of 176,854, is the capital of the Punjab; Allahabad, with a population of 175,246, is the capital of the North-Western Provinces; and Nagpur, with 117,014 souls, is the capital of the Central Provinces. There are other cities, even more populous than those just mentioned, such as Lucknow, Benares, and Delhi, but they do not take rank as capitals of British provinces. In all of these and many others municipal institutions have been granted by the British government, in order that their citizens may share with government the burdens and glory of the British empire, of which they are a part.

22. **A Retrospect.** In looking back at the past, the

reader can realize one change which has taken place. The capital cities of former dynasties were fortified and securely placed in the interior of the country, as at Delhi, Mandalay, Hyderabad in Sindh, Lahore, Poona, Bijapur, and other stations which will occur to the reader. They were planted where their rulers wished, and they received sometimes favours and at others severe treatment. The inhabitants were either drawn to the city by a lavish expenditure of imperial funds, or else held there by force, and forbidden to leave it if they wished to go. Under British rule cities may grow up just where they please, and the residents may go wherever they desire. The public taxes drawn from the rural population of the villages are not lavished on them. Their citizens pay local rates as well as public taxes, and the representatives of the people administer the local taxation. It will be observed that the capital cities of British India have grown up wherever that is possible on the sea coast, or on a tidal river where trade can reach them by water, and where the arm of England can best protect them. A well-known poet, Campbell, has explained the objects of this selection in the following stirring lines:

"Britannia needs no bulwarks,
No towers along the steep;
Her march is o'er the mountain-waves,
Her home is on the deep.
With thunders from her native oak
She quells the floods below—
As they roar on the shore,
When the stormy winds do blow."

CHAPTER III.

THE DISTRICT.

23. **Centres of Life.** Every village and town in India forms a part of some district, and there is no intelligent inhabitant of either who cannot tell you the name of his own district. Having gained this step in learning something about his country, the citizen of India ought to take an interest in knowing more about the government of the district. When one hears that in British India alone the villages and towns number 537,901, it may seem difficult for a single village to grasp the idea that it is a part of the empire. The mind is oppressed by a sense of numbers, and by the very small part which one village fills in the whole collection. But with the districts this is not the case. Including Aden and six districts in Berar, which for different reasons might have been excluded, the census of 1891 enumerates 250 districts in the whole of British India. This number, however, excludes Calcutta and its suburbs, although it includes Bombay. But whether the number of districts should be stated as 244 or 251, the result is practically the same. The full importance of the district is at once felt when

we know that about 250 of them make up the whole of India outside the native states. The district is a portion of the empire which every one can readily appreciate, and for this reason it is generally described as the centre of life in the Indian empire. It is in the district that we see the great machine of government at work, and by its results there we can, to a large extent, estimate its success. If the machine works well at this vital centre, the whole empire is probably well governed. Cities, and even provinces, appear and disappear from the map, but the districts have on the whole preserved their names through the many changes of rule through which India has passed.

24. **Parts of the Province.** At the same time, important as the Indian district is, it remains but a part of the province or empire, from whose fortunes it cannot detach itself. It is therefore impossible to form a correct judgment regarding the treatment of any particular locality without bearing in mind that the interests of one district, and those of others or of the whole province may at times be opposed to each other. It is the government of the empire, or that of the province, which must hold the balance between conflicting interests when they arise. We must not at once infer from any loss suffered by one district that the government is to blame. There may be an absolute necessity for the sacrifice of some local claims in order to protect the greater and wider interests of the whole nation. For instance, in the old days former rulers of Indian provinces permitted disorder and violence in their frontier districts in order to discourage their neighbours from entering their territories. The outer fringe of the kingdom

was sacrificed for the interior. In one corner of the Punjab a jaghir was conferred upon Karim-ud-din, Khan of Chamkanni by the Sikhs in return for twenty Afridi heads, which he was expected to produce every year. On the extreme eastern frontier of India there is still a settlement of wild Was, or head-hunters, who, under the Mandalay government, excited such terror as to prevent the immigration of Chinese bands into the Shan states. The British government adopts no such methods for defending India from invasion, or from the inroads of plundering gangs. But there are ways in which the residents of one locality are at times called upon to suffer loss for the gain of others. When the Kushmore embankment was made to protect Jacobabad and parts of the Sukkur district from the floods of the Indus its effect was to exclude some tracts of land in Jacobabad from the overflow of the river's waters which they needed for cultivation. The loss of the cultivation on that frontier of Sindh was serious, but the gains of a more numerous population further west outweighed the sacrifice. It was necessary to injure the few in the interests of the many. Whilst then it is correct to regard the district as the centre of the real life of India, and to look there for traces of prosperity and good rule, we must not forget that at times the losses or injury of one district may prove necessary for the good of others.

25. **Area of the District.** In parcelling out a country into counties or districts, the object of a good ruler is to give to each district-officer an equally onerous charge. Yet it is evident that the districts vary much in size and population in the different provinces. The average size and population of the British dis-

tricts, after excluding the four cities described in the last chapter, is 3,875 square miles and 880,965 persons. But in Madras these figures are largely exceeded, and 1,466,000 persons and 5,882 square miles form the average district. In Bombay outside Sindh the average area is 4,292 square miles, and in Sindh it is 9,558 square miles. The North-Western Provinces have the smallest average of area, 2,194 square miles, but an average population to the district of nearly one million souls. In Bengal the population of the districts averages one-and-a-half millions. How are these differences explained? Much depends upon the two conditions just noticed, area and population. The district must be under one head, who is responsible for its government, and a single officer cannot cover more than a certain area of inspection and control. Again, in a smaller area he cannot do his duty by too vast a population. Much also depends upon the character of the people, their neighbours, and the land-tenure. If the people are turbulent, or if their neighbours are badly governed or savage tribes, the district officer's attention is distracted by disorderly classes, or by the affairs of his neighbours. His police arrangements involve more care and time. So too, the extent of his revenue duties depends largely upon the number of his rent-paying landlords. The Benares division of the North-Western Provinces is larger in area and population than the Agra division. But the former has five districts with 29 subdivisions, while for Agra six districts and 48 subdivisions are needed. The land-revenue of Benares is less than 50 lakhs, while that of Agra exceeds 80 lakhs, and in the former much is paid directly into the treasury by large landlords, whereas in Agra the small cultivators are more numerous. Consequently, the districts in Agra require larger establishments. The differences in size and population of the districts of British India are to be accounted for by these distinctions. As far as possible, the charge of each district represents an equal responsibility.

26. **The Executive.** The district officers are the most important executive officers of government. They carry out or "execute" the commands of law and of government. Above them are officers who control, supervise, or issue orders. But the district officials, namely the collector and his assistants, the judge and his subordinate courts, the superintendent of police, the executive engineer with his assistants, and the district surgeon constitute the officials upon whom the government relies to give effect to its orders or to administer the law. They are the chief wheels in the machine of government, and their names are familiar to all the villages and towns in their districts. Upon their integrity, capacity, and energy depends the success of government. The system of the central government may be quite excellent, but if the district officers are inefficient, its benefits would never reach the masses of the district population. The sphere of duties entrusted to the executive of a district is very wide. They preserve order and maintain the public peace, they administer criminal and civil justice, they collect the public revenue and decide land disputes, they propose and carry out public works, administer famine relief, and watch over the public health. They not only manage the affairs entrusted to them, but they also control the working of municipal and other local

self-governing bodies. To them the population of the districts look in all their troubles and difficulties, and through them the people learn the intentions and wishes of the provincial and the supreme governments. They are not merely the mouth but the eyes and ears of government. The legislative machine which makes or alters laws is not entrusted to them, but their reports are the spring which, under the direction of the governors of provinces, sets the legislative wheel in motion. The expenditure of public funds is entrusted to them, the jails and schools are visited by them, and any defects are duly brought by them to the notice of the departments concerned.

27. **The Collector.** The chief of the whole district staff is the collector, although in his own sphere of duty the district judge is independent of him. In arranging for the proper conduct of affairs in the district, government have to keep two objects in view—unity and economy. When the British took over the districts from the rulers who preceded them there was no distinction drawn between judicial and executive duties. The native governments ruled absolutely, and such powers as they entrusted to their district officers were exercised without much control; an entire unity of purpose was thus secured. There were no written laws providing for the creation of municipalities or for the establishment of courts or the collection of taxes. To the present day there are in the native states no bodies working independently of the executive, to whom is entrusted the power of making laws. The ruling chiefs issue their commands, and their commands are the law. The British government was the first to introduce into India the principle of

making executive officers subordinate to the law, and of entrusting to a body, separate from the provincial government, the task of making laws which the government itself and its officers must respect and obey. As soon as the country had really settled down to peace, and civil government was firmly established, the functions of chief executive officer and chief judge in the district were separated. Accordingly in every settled district there is a collector and a judge, to the former of whom is committed the chief executive command, and to the latter the chief judicial authority. But with this exception unity and economy are served by making the collector head of the several departments in his district. The collector is not merely the officer who is responsible for the collection of the land revenue and the taxes, he is also the district magistrate, and the chief local officer who controls the operations of the police and, if necessary, invokes the aid of the military forces. In short, he is responsible for order and public peace. He is also responsible for the public welfare, and has a powerful voice in determining what roads and public works are needed, what sanitary measures are required, and where and when self-government should be extended to the towns. He is often registrar of deeds, and inspector of factories, and generally he is the pivot upon which the local authority of government revolves. If anything goes wrong, it is the duty of the collector to correct the mischief if he can do so, and, if not, to report it to the proper authority.

28. **Subdivisions.** Beneath the collector are several officers who are responsible for the government of portions of his district called subdivisions, generally a group

of "Tahsils" or "Talukas." These subdivisions are liable to more frequent changes of area than are the districts. At present there are 1056 subdivisions into which the 250 districts enumerated in the last census are divided. The chain of authority and responsibility is by them extended throughout the villages of British India, and the principle of unity is preserved. Above the district there is usually an officer of control and supervision, who has authority over several districts. He is called a commissioner, and his sphere of control is styled a division. There are 54 divisions in the territory classed by the census as British India, but in Madras there are no commissioners, their functions being taken by a central board of revenue. The commissioners differ from the collectors or district chiefs in this important respect, that they are officers of control rather than men of action. The real centre of active and direct authority lies in the districts, and the main fact to be borne in mind is that British India is divided by the census returns into 12 provinces or administrations, forming 250 districts which, as already explained, exclude one city and include the Berars and Aden.

29. **District Appointments.** It is evident that the utmost care is needed in the selection of collectors or chiefs of the Indian districts. Their powers are considerable, and no pains must be spared to select the best men that can be got. Ability, good character, and personal knowledge of the principles upon which British administration is conducted are the three main qualifications. Every Indian subject of the Queen Empress has exactly the same right as her subjects living in the United Kingdom, or in the colonies and dependencies of the Crown, to compete for the Civil Service

of India, from whose ranks men are chosen for the office of collector. An annual examination is held at the centre of the empire in London, at which all candidates from all quarters of the British Empire, who have satisfied the tests prescribed as to age and nationality and proof of good moral character, may compete for the Indian Civil Service. The same papers are set to all, and the same time is allowed for their answers. The candidate's name does not appear upon his answers, and the examiners only know him by a number, so that they cannot tell who is the author of the papers which they have to mark. Those who get the highest marks obtain the reward of being selected as candidates, and after a short period of probation in England and further examination they are enrolled, if finally successful, in the Civil Service of India. By their residence in England candidates who may have lived in other parts of the British Empire acquire some personal knowledge of the institutions and public life of the country on whose behalf they are sent to conduct the British administration of India. At present the number of civil servants so selected and serving in India is 1003, including the natives of India who have succeeded in the public competition. After their enlistment in the ranks of the Civil Service the selected candidates are trained in the various grades and departments of that service, and when qualified for the posts they are appointed to be district judges or district collectors. No European subject of the Queen Empress can attain to the rank of collector except by means of this public competition, but in the case of natives of India power has been taken by an Act of Parliament to appoint them by direct selection, although they may have failed to win an appointment by means of competitive examination. At present there are 44 native civil servants so appointed. They used to be called statutory civilians.

30. **Subdivisional Appointments.** In the subdivisions of districts the British government to a very large extent employs natives of India. In this respect its practice differs from that of other European countries, such as France or Russia, which possess territories in Asia. A recent traveller in Transcaspia, a province in Central Asia under the dominion of Russia, writes in a paper read before the Society of Arts in London on the 1st of April, 1897, as follows: "Every one of these posts of high office in the civil and military administration in Transcaspia and Turkestan, with the exception of one inspectorship of police, is held by a Russian; nay more, not only are the natives excluded from the post of subdivisional officer, corresponding to Tahsildar or Mamlatdar which in India is invariably held by a native, but the subdivisional officer's staff, with assistant secretary and two clerks, are all Russians. The only post held by natives in the civil administration are those of interpreters to the governors, and in the various offices one or two have been appointed *pristavs*. They are absolutely excluded from all share in the executive government. The state of things in the army is the same. In Turkestan as in Transcaspia there is no native army, and there is not a single native in the Russian army of occupation." In contrast with this state of affairs, it is interesting to compare the progress made in India during the last twenty-five years in the increased employment of the natives. The example of one

province will suffice. If you turn to the civil list of Bombay in 1872, you will find a list of 37 deputy collectors and magistrates, of whom 11 were Europeans. In the same list there were 83 subordinate judges, of whom 5 were Europeans. In January, 1897, there were 51 deputy collectors in the same divisions of the province. of whom 4 were Europeans, while out of 103 subordinate judges there was only 1 European. The Mamlatdars in 1897 were without exception natives of India. In short, the administration of India is only controlled and supervised by a limited number of British officers, while the vast bulk of the civil appointments are held by the natives. The experiment is one which is watched by foreign nations with some degree of wonder. but it has always been a declared aim of the British government to teach the people of India to administer their own affairs in accordance with those principles of justice, integrity, and public duty which are required by public opinion in the United Kingdom. The association of a few hundred British officials chosen by competition in England, with several thousands of natives in the work of administration is the means by which it is sought to achieve this end.

CHAPTER IV.

THE PROVINCES.

31. **Akbar's Subahs.** Rulers have constantly changed in the course of Indian history, and invaders have come and gone, but the names and sites of villages and even the arrangements of districts have survived dynastic changes. The case has been different with the divisions of the country into provinces. The thirteen provinces into which India is to-day divided, and which are marked on the maps used in all quarters of the globe, are a matter of modern creation. For many centuries the broad division of the country into Hindustan and the Dekhan answered all purposes. By Hindustan was indicated the basins of the great rivers Indus and the Ganges with their affluents, whilst the Dekhan signified the country, more or less known, lying to the south of the Satpuras. It was not until the firm rule of Akbar had knit together the north and the south and the east and the west under one empire, that the provinces took shape, and the villages and districts of India became familiar with the titles of the provincial governors who administered their affairs. It requires

some advance in the settlement of a country and in

THE EMPEROR AKBAR

its peaceful submission to a central authority before it can be mapped out into well recognized provinces.

When civil disorder reigns villages may survive, but the boundaries of subahs or provinces are readily lost and ignored. In the reign of Akbar the time was suitable for creating provinces, and Abul Fazl Allámi, author of the *Aín-i Akbari*, gives the following account: "In the fortieth[1] year of the divine era, his Majesty's dominions consisted of 105 Sarkárs or divisions of Súbahs, and 2737 townships. His Majesty divided the empire into 12 provinces called Súbahs, and when Berar, Khandesh, and Ahmednagar were conquered their number was fixed at fifteen." He then gives a full account of these 12 provinces, namely—Bengal, Behar, Allahabad, Oudh, Agra, Malwa, Guzerat, Ajmir, Delhi, Lahore, Multan, and Kabul.

32. **British Provinces.** The very names of the 13 provinces of India under British administration indicate some of the changes which have taken place. They are Madras, Bombay, Bengal, North-Western Provinces, Punjab, Central Provinces, Assam, Burma, Ajmir, the Berars, Coorg, Baluchistan, and the Andamans. But there are differences between the Moghal and the British systems which do not lie on the surface. One can see at a glance that Akbar's India included Kabul, a term which embraced Kashmir, Swat, Bajaur, and Kandahar, and that British India, although contracted on the west, is to-day extended on the east as far as the river Mekong. Nor can one fail to notice in reading the names of the provinces that the effective control of the Imperial government over the south and south-west of India is greater than it was four centuries ago. But an essential difference

[1] A.D. 1594-95.

between Akbar's and the present provincial arrangements of the Indian Empire lies in the modern practice of excluding the native states from the provinces of the empire. Under Akbar's rule Mewar and Marwar were integral parts of the province of Ajmir, Baroda was a sarkar of Guzerat, Udaipur, Ratlam, and Dhar were included in the province of Malwa, and Indore was a part of Berar. In short, the Empire of Delhi treated the native states as a part of Moghal India, whilst under British rule three-eighths of India, or, some 600,000 square miles, are scrupulously excluded from the British provinces, and thus preserved against the risk of annexation or encroachment. How the British provinces took shape must yet be told, but before that point is reached a few words are needed in order to explain the expressions local government and local administration.

33. **Titles of the Provinces.** It is very probable that the limits of some of the British Indian provinces may be altered. They vary considerably in size, from small Coorg with an area of 1583 square miles, to Burma with its territory of 171,430 square miles, and in population the differences are still more striking. Each of them is under a local chief, but his title varies from governor to lieutenant governor or chief commissioner. Two—Madras and Bombay—are under governors, and are often called presidencies, because the governor, who is sent out from England for a term of five years, presides over a council which consists of himself and two councillors. Four—Bengal, North-Western Provinces, Punjab, and Burma—are local governments, under lieutenant governors chosen by the Viceroy. In these six provinces there are two features common to all. The

presidencies and local governments are given a sum of money out of the public purse over which they exercise large powers, and there are in all of them councils for making laws and regulations. The seven remaining provinces are called local administrations. Three small provinces—Berar, Ajmir, and Coorg—are administered under the more direct control of the Imperial government by officers who also hold political offices. Two—the Central Provinces and Assam—are under chief commissioners, and differ but little from the local governments under lieutenant governors, from which some of these districts were originally detached. The two remaining provinces of India are British Baluchistan and the penal settlement of the Andaman Islands. It will be observed that no attempt is made to divide India into equal provinces. There is no apparent method followed in fixing their limits, and the reason for this is to be found in the circumstances under which British rule gradually grew up in the country. The English company never dreamt of empire when they began to trade with India. They avoided war and any increase of responsibilities as much as possible. But events were too strong for them, and the provinces took their shape not out of any design, but under the pressure of self-defence and out of accidents which were never foreseen. In order that the provincial arrangement may be properly understood, it is necessary to look back at the course of events.

34. Madras. The Madras province or presidency is the oldest of British Indian provinces. A petty chief sold to a British trading company in 1639 the site of Fort St. George, because he expected much profit by trading with them. In 1653 this humble settlement, acquired so lawfully and peacefully, was made a presidency, but a century later it was violently captured by the French.

LORD CLIVE.

From an engraving by Bartolozzi, after the picture by Nathaniel Dance.

After its restoration the tide of war turned, and Masulipatam was taken from the French in 1757, and eight years later the emperor of Delhi Shah Alam, granted the Northern Sarkars to Clive The French in course of time opened negotiations with the neighbouring native chiefs, hoping with their aid to expel the British settlers, and a Mahomedan general in the service of the Hindu state of Mysore, named Hyder Ali, who had usurped his master's power, lent a ready ear to their proposals. The result of the Mysore wars which ensued with Hyder Ali and his son Tippu Sultan was to restore the Hindu dynasty to power in Mysore, and to add five districts to the Madras Presidency. Two more districts were ceded by the Nizam of Hyderabad, and Kurnool was added in 1838. By that year the province of Madras was completed, but in 1862 its government transferred to Bombay the northern district of North Canara. Thus from a quiet trading settlement Madras grew under the three influences of wars with the French, grants from the emperor, and the defeat of the Mysore usurper, into a settled province of British India, embracing an area of 141,189 square miles, with 35½ millions of people.

35. **Bombay.** Only twenty-six years before the Hindu raja invited the British traders to Madras, a British factory had been established on the western coast at Surat under a firman granted by the emperor of Delhi, who in the next year, 1614 issued orders to allow the merchants of King James the privileges of free trade throughout his empire. Within twenty years of the cession of Bombay by the Portuguese to the King of England, the head-quarters of the trading company were moved from Surat to that island, and in 1708 the settlement was made a presidency. The British occupation of Bombay was thus founded upon

a just title. But the British settlers were hemmed in on all sides by the Maratha government, which subsequently became established at Poona. The rise of Sivaji to power commenced after the establishment of the company at Surat, and for a century the British merchants gained little profit from the emperor's firman in favour of free trade. In consequence of a revolution at Poona which followed the murder of the Peshwa Narain Rao, the usurper Raghoba applied to the British for aid, and ceded to them Bassein, Salsette, and other islands near Bombay. The interference of the British on behalf of Raghoba led to their defeat at Wurgaon and consequently to further hostilities. It was impossible for either party to sheath the sword until one side or the other prevailed, and fresh treaties only paved the way for fresh wars. Surat, Broach, and Kaira were acquired by force of arms in the second Maratha war, and after the battle of Kirkee, in 1817, the Dekhan and the Konkan were added to the presidency. In 1843 Sindh was annexed by Sir Charles Napier, and the fort of Aden in Arabia, which was captured in 1839, was handed over to Bombay, of which province it was afterwards declared to be an integral part. Thus the history of Madras was repeated in the case of Bombay, a province of 125,144 square miles with nearly 19 millions of people.

36. **Bengal.** The growth of Bengal was far more rapid. In Madras and Bombay the company acquired a legal title to only small settlements on the sea coast. The growth of the factory into a province was the slow result of a struggle on the part of the settlers to retain in peace a strip of coast which belonged to them of right. The French and Hyder Ali in the south, and the Mara-

thas in the Dekhan, threatened to drive the British traders into the sea, and their resistance and the victories won by them over their assailants brought to them the spoils of war. In Bengal the same company of London merchants, who had commenced their trade in Surat, acquired from the Delhi emperor a right to trade with Pipli in the Midnapur district. But no factory was established until 1642, when Balasor was selected. The native authorities oppressed the foreign traders, and seized their factories when they prepared to defend themselves. The company accordingly obtained the permission of the local governor of Bengal in 1698 to purchase Calcutta, and for some time their affairs prospered. But in 1756 the Subahdar of Bengal, Suraj-ad-Daula, attacked Calcutta, and on the 5th of August in that year he thrust 146 Englishmen into the "Black Hole," where all save 23 perished in a single night. The settlement thus lost to the company was recaptured on 2nd January, 1757, by a force sent to its relief under Clive from Madras. Soon afterwards the battle of Plassey was fought and won on the 23rd of June, and in 1765 the emperor, Shah Alam, conferred the Diwani of Bengal, Behar, and Orissa upon the East India Company. The company thus acquired by a single stroke a large territory. In 1803 Orissa proper was conquered from the Marathas, who had invaded it without any lawful pretext, and the whole province of British Bengal, which then included part of the present North-Western Provinces, was placed under the administration of the Governor General of Bengal until 1834, in which year the Governor General of Bengal became Governor General of India. The Governor General of India, however, continued, without the aid

CALCUTTA, FROM THE OUCHTERLONY MONUMENT, LOOKING NORTH-WEST.

of his council, to govern the province until 1854, in which year the first Lieutenant Governor of Bengal was appointed. In 1836 the upper provinces were detached from Bengal and added to the province which was afterwards called the North-Western Provinces, while Bengal itself received, in 1850, some tracts from Sikkim, and in 1865 further additions from Bhutan. Again, in 1874, it became necessary to relieve the local government of an excessive charge by detaching the districts now known as the province of Assam. Bengal however remains the second in point of area, and the first in respect of population, of the provinces of the empire, embracing 151,543 square miles with more than 71 millions of people. Its capital is Calcutta.

British rule in Bengal was thus established over the whole province upon the best of titles. The defence of the settlement of Calcutta and the vindication of its lawful claims, after the outrage of the "Black Hole," were followed by the emperor's firman which conferred upon the British merchants the rights and duties of governing the province. The extent of the emperor's grant was so large that it included not merely the province of Bengal as now known and Assam, but it laid the foundations of the adjoining province, which has next to be described.

37. **The North-Western Provinces.** The very name which this province still bears throws light upon the policy which the British company desired to pursue. When Bengal was granted to the British, its population rapidly grew rich and prosperous under their rule. Unfortunately the country beyond it remained a prey to anarchy and civil war. The merchants who

had acquired Bengal had no wish to extend their responsibilities, but in order to protect their possessions they were drawn into wars with the Marathas, and then with the Nepalese They had created a kingdom of Oudh in the hope that a strong and friendly power might prove a good neighbour, and protect its own as well as the company's frontier from attack. The king of Oudh disappointed their hopes, and the armies of Sindhia and Holkar took the field against a British force under Lord Lake. The results of the arrangements made with Oudh, and of the defeat of the Marathas, were the cession and conquest of certain districts which were called the "ceded and conquered districts." The war with Nepal added to them some hill-tracts, and two years later an attack upon the residency at Sitabaldi led to the deposition of the ruler of Nagpur, and a further addition of some southern districts to those previously ceded or conquered. The final break up of Oudh linked that state to the districts mentioned. and after the mutiny the North-Western Provinces transferred the Sagar and Nerbada territories to a new province in the south called the Central Province, and handed over Delhi to the Punjab. The seat of its government was moved from Agra to Allahabad. For many years the province, which in Akbar's reign was called Allahabad, bore the brunt of frontier defence, and grew in strength under the attacks of enemies from all sides. It is now placed under a lieutenant governor, and it still retains its old title although the real north-western frontier is far removed from its extreme limits. Its area is 107,503 square miles with 47 millions of people.

38. **The Punjab.** The province of Punjab, watered

by the five rivers—the Sutlej, Beas, Ravi, Chenab, and Jhelum—was created almost at a single step, like that of Bengal. It was not laboriously built up like the North-Western Provinces out of a long series of wars. The reason for this was that for many years the British company strove hard to avoid an extension of its rule beyond the north-western boundary. Accordingly, the same policy which had been tried in Oudh, when Oudh was recognized as a native kingdom, was applied on a larger scale to the Punjab. In 1809 the company made a treaty with Ranjit Singh which left to that conquering ruler of the Sikhs the country beyond the Sutlej. Ranjit Singh reduced the Punjab to order by annexing the native states within it, and by maintaining a powerful army. The army got beyond the control of its leaders, and in 1845 it numbered 72,000 men with 381 guns. On 13th December of that year the Governor General published a proclamation in which he laid stress on the fact that the treaty of 1809 had been faithfully observed by the British government, which "sincerely desired to see a strong Sikh government re-established in the Punjab able to control its army and to protect its subjects." But the Sikhs had nevertheless invaded British territory "without a shadow of provocation." To punish this violation of treaty the territories of Dhulip Singh, who had succeeded to his father, Ranjit Singh, were annexed, and subsequent victories led to the annexation of the rest in 1849. The country was first governed by a Board of three members, and then in 1853 by a chief commissioner. In 1859 it was placed under a lieutenant governor. Its area is now 110,667 square miles, with a population of nearly 21 millions. Its chief city is Lahore.

39. **The Central Provinces.** It has been shown that from the North-Western Provinces certain districts were detached, namely the Sagar provinces, conquered from Sindhia, and the Narbada provinces, acquired from the Raja of Nagpur in 1818. When the Raja of Nagpur, Raghoji III. died without heirs in 1853, the rest of his territories were added to these two groups of provinces. In 1860 the upper Godaveri district ceded by the Nizam, and the Nimar district given up by Sindhia in the course of certain exchanges of territory between the British government and the rulers of Hyderabad and Gwalior, were combined with the rest of the central districts, and one united province was made and placed under a chief commissioner in 1861. The area of the 18 districts so combined is 86,501 square miles, with nearly 11 millions of people. The capital town is Nagpur

40. **Assam.** Part of this province, created in 1874, was severed from Bengal, and two of its districts, Sylhet and Goalpura, were included in the emperor's Diwani grant of 1765 already referred to. Other districts, including that which gives its name to the province, were conquered from the Burmese in 1826, and portions of the hill districts, inhabited by wild and lawless people, were annexed from time to time, as a punishment to the tribes for their attacks upon villages within the British border. The area of the whole charge placed under a chief commissioner is 49,004 square miles, with a population of about five and a half millions. The capital town is Shillong. There is not a single town, in the whole of Assam, which has a population of 20,000 inhabitants.

41. **Burma.** The British authorities were even

more anxious to avoid an increase of their responsibilities on the north-eastern frontier than in the Punjab on the north-west. If the issues of peace or war had rested entirely with them, the court at Ava would still be ruling over Burma But the constant insults and encroachments of the Burmese authorities thrice compelled the British to draw the sword in defence of their rights, and on the 1st of January, 1886, Upper and Lower Burma were united, and became a province of the Indian empire. It will be remembered that the emperor's grant of Bengal to the company brought their districts of Assam and Chittagong into close touch with the province of Arakan The King of Burma conquered Arakan in 1784, and some forty years later the Burmese government advanced a claim to the sovereignty of Bengal as far as Murshedabad. The company's territories were violated, and when Lord Amherst, the governor-general, addressed the King of Ava in serious tones of remonstrance, he replied that "it is the pleasure of the king of the white elephant, the lord of the seas and land, that no further communication be sent to the golden feet." Only one answer was possible to so impudent a refusal to discuss the matters at issue. As the result of the war which followed, the lower provinces of Arakan, Tavoy, and Tenasserim were ceded in 1826 to the company, and an agreement was concluded with the Burmese for the protection of the company's trade.

The treaty was not kept, and in 1852 an insult, deliberately offered by the governor of Rangoon to Captain Fishbourne, led to the capture of that city, and the annexation of Pegu by Lord Dalhousie. Finally, after a long course of most unsatisfactory conduct toward the British representative, King Thibau proclaimed in November, 1885, his intention of invading Lower Burma, and war was of necessity declared

THE MARQUESS OF DUFFERIN AND AVA, K.P., 1884 TO 1888.
From a photograph by Bourne & Shepherd, Calcutta.

which ended in the annexation of Upper Burma by Lord Dufferin. In 1862 the lower provinces had been placed under a chief commissioner, and in 1897 both Upper and Lower Burma were united under a lieutenant-governor, whose head-quarters are at Rangoon. The eastern frontiers of the Indian empire now touch Siam on the south, the French possessions on the Mekong, and the empire of China on the north. Exclusive of the Shan states, the area of the province is 171,430 square miles, with a population of seven and a half millions. In area therefore the province, which includes 36 districts, is the largest of Indian provinces, and since the country was the scene of constant disorders, which desolated the villages and reduced the population during the rule of the Avan court, it is certain that under the influences of peace and order its population will greatly increase. The port of Rangoon, protected by British command of the seas, already takes its place as one of the large centres of trade and commerce under the British flag.

42. **Five Remaining Provinces.** A very brief account of the remaining provinces will suffice to complete this review of the growth of the present Indian empire. Ajmir with Merwara is in Rajputana. Ajmir was received from Sindhia in 1818 in exchange for certain territories which had been acquired from the Peshwa. Merwara fell to the company as its share of a district rescued from gangs of plunderers by a British force sent to assist the Rajput states of Mewar and Marwar. The chief political officer in Rajputana is also the chief commissioner of Ajmir.

The Berars, lying between two ranges of hills in the centre of India on the road from Bombay to Nagpur, were assigned to the British by the Nizam for the punctual payment of a force which the ruler of Hyderabad has engaged by treaty to maintain. Its six districts, with an area of 17,718 square miles and a population of 2,879,040, are included in the census as a province of British India because the entire administration is vested in the government of India. But the province is not strictly a part of British India as defined by law.

Coorg, a small province covering 1,582 square miles, nestles in the hills which bound the Mysore state on the west The cruelties inflicted on his subjects by its ruler, Vira Rajendra Wadiar, induced the people to seek the protection of the company, and when war was declared in 1834 and the district conquered, it was formally annexed by Lord William Bentinck "at the unanimous wish of the inhabitants." Its capital is Mercara, and the resident of Mysore administers the province as a chief commissioner in accordance with the wishes of the Coorgis, who asked that their country might be treated as a separate province.

British Baluchistan, with an area of 18,020 square miles, is an advanced outpost of the empire on the south of Afghanistan, and is administered by the chief commissioner and chief political officer at Quetta. The district of Quetta came under British rule in 1879, the Bori valley in 1884, and the Zhob district in 1889.

The Andamans, with Port Blair as their head-quarters, were established as the penal settlement for Indian convicts in 1858 They form a group of islands on the south-east side of Bengal about 600 miles from the mouth of the Hughli.

43. **Little Seeds.** The rapid expansion of British rule in India is due to the growth of a few seeds of

peace, law, and commerce, planted on the coasts of the country by a company of merchants. Under the shade of these plantations the settlements of Bombay, Surat, Calcutta, and Madras grew into cities, and neighbouring districts and states, wearied by constant strife, sought the protection of the strong men from over the seas who showed that they were able to restore to the people of India the peace and order which they so much needed. The public enemies, who carried fire and sword through the land, and left the districts half deserted and the villages in flames, could not be suppressed by the unaided efforts of the Indians themselves. Mr. Tupper relates of the district of Karnal in the Punjab that out of 221 villages in one part of it, the inhabitants of 178 were absolutely driven from their homes and lands in the beginning of the present century. Similar instances could be mentioned in Central India. Habits of law and peace were lost in the incessant appeal to arms. The harassed people, therefore, welcomed a power which could restore rest to the land, and give security to its industrious raiyats. No one, least of all the British traders, expected or wished for empire when they opened trade with India. But the example, set by the first fugitives who fled to Bombay, and by the state of Coorg was followed by others who saw that the only hope for their own country lay in a close alliance with a race able to teach the Indian people how to fight and to defeat anarchy and lawlessness.

"Our enemies have fall'n, have fall'n: the seed,
The little seed they laughed at in the dark
Has risen and cleft the soil, and grown a bulk
Of spanless girth that lays on every side
A thousand arms and rushes to the sun."

CHAPTER V.

THE NATIVE STATES.

44. **Foreign Territory.** If the reader who has reached this point in his studies should consult a map of India he would notice considerable tracts of country which are not included in the districts or the provinces hitherto described. Some of these tracts are filled by a cluster of important states lying close to each other; others form single principalities under one chief, and others again lie scattered about in small patches within the ring fence of a British district. The total area occupied by them is not much less than a half of that of British India, and the number of separate states within this area is nearly eight hundred. Some are very large, and others can count only a few villages. But there is one feature common to all. Although they are all parts of India or of the British empire in India, yet they are not parts of the territories governed by the British which are known as British India. They are not ruled by the officers of the Queen Empress, although they are protected by Her Majesty. British courts of law have no jurisdiction in them or over them so far as their general population is con-

cerned. The people who reside in them are subjects of the chiefs, and in short the states are not British, but foreign territory.

It does not follow, however, that the citizen of British India need take no account of them, or regard them as no concern of his. On the contrary, past experience has shown that the good government of the native states, and the prosperity of their subjects, are objects of direct interest to the British government and its citizens. If disorder should gain head in one of the great blocks of territory filled by several states, such as the Central India Agency, it would be impossible to exclude it from the adjoining provinces. This lesson was taught by the Pindari war. If the native army should defy its officers as the armies of Gwalior and the Punjab once did, the battles of Maharajpur and Sobraon would have to be repeated. Again, if a powerful ruler were to enter into negotiations with the enemies of Great Britain, as Tippu Sultan once did with the French, war both by sea and land might again be provoked, and it might involve not only the ruin of the state but great losses to British India. So too in the affairs of every day: if the chiefs who rule the patches of foreign territory in British districts should shelter gangs of robbers or encourage practices like suttee and infanticide, which are forbidden in the neighbouring British villages their action would defeat the efforts of British law and peace. The friendly and neighbourly conduct of the native chiefs is therefore essential both to the welfare of British India and to the continuance of the native states.

45. **Past and Present.** There is no achievement of which the British government is more proud than the

preservation of so many states in the midst of its territories. Before the establishment of British rule the states were either annexed by a stronger power, as by the emperor of Delhi, or by the Sikh Lion of the Punjab, Ranjit Singh, or else they were left in a state of chronic disturbance and civil war as in Central India. The alternative in old days lay between absorption and anarchy. Even after the successful wars which the British company waged in defence of its factories in Surat, Madras, Calcutta, and Bombay, the difficulty of transforming the princes and chiefs of the states into loyal neighbours and allies was so great as to seem a hopeless task, and it required many changes of policy. Success has, however, been attained by a resolute adherence to a principle which was expressed by a Secretary of State for India in these terms, written in 1860: "It is not by the extension of our empire that its permanence is to be secured, but by the character of British rule in the territories already committed to our care, and by showing that we are as willing to respect the rights of others as we are capable of maintaining our own."

46. **Lord Cornwallis.** The first step taken by the company with the intention of preserving the native states had to be retraced. It ended in failure and continual wars. The British traders, who had obtained the emperor's sanads and had proceeded peacefully and lawfully to establish their factories on the sea coast, had neither the desire nor the idea of exchanging commerce for rule. Their first object was to engage in profitable trade, not to take part in intrigues and wars. When they were forced by attacks to defend themselves and to strengthen their positions,

the English parliament did all in its power to restrain them from undertaking larger responsibilities. Accordingly, in the reign of George III. an Act was passed in 1793, which recited the words that "to pursue schemes of conquest and extension of dominion are measures repugnant to the wish, the honour, and the policy of this nation." The authorities at home tried to carry out this view, and they forbade their officers in India to enter into any engagements with the native states which could be avoided. In pursuance of these orders Lord Cornwallis not only refused to protect chiefs who asked for the British alliance, but he even cancelled some treaties into which his predecessors and the government of Bombay had been drawn. His policy was one of not intervening in the affairs of the chiefs who were constantly at war with each other. The result was that civil war spread like a jungle fire, and the British districts were overrun by bands of armed robbers who found a shelter in foreign territory.

47. **Lord Hastings.** It devolved upon Lord Moira, better known as Lord Hastings, who filled the post of Governor-General from 1813 for ten years, to conduct to a successful issue the wars which the policy of "let alone" entailed, and as a consequence to bring the greater part of the native states under British protection. Wars ceased between the native princes and the company, and between one prince and another. The conditions of a lasting settlement were laid down, and from that date the relations between the states and the provinces were put upon a satisfactory basis. But for many years it was considered proper to leave the rulers of the protected states entirely to themselves in the management of their internal affairs.

The consequence was that, for lack of timely advice and interference, misrule grew to serious proportions; and then, when the ruling chief chanced to die without leaving an heir, public opinion demanded a change of rulers, and the state was held to have lapsed to British rule.

48. **Lord Canning.** When the government of India was transferred in 1858 to the crown an end was put to these lapses, and the ruling princes were assured of the desire of Her Majesty to continue the dignity and representation of their houses. As long as they are loyal to the crown and faithful to their engagements, the chiefs are assured that they will be protected and their states perpetuated. Advice is given to them when needed, and if any particular chief is proved to be unfit for rule he is replaced by another who can govern better. The states themselves are both protected and preserved. Advantage is taken of minorities or any temporary removal of the chief to introduce a better system, as was done in Mysore and Baroda, but when reforms have been carried out the native state reverts to the rule of its own chief. By these means an enormous area of 595,167 square miles has been preserved under native rule in the teeth of many difficulties.

49. **Classes of States.** What these difficulties have been may be more readily understood if a general idea is formed of the position of the states, and of the points upon which differences would naturally arise between them and their powerful neighbour. The states protected by the government of India may be divided into three classes: those which lie close to each other, and form extensive blocks of territory subject to

GEORGE CANNING, 1827. Bust in National Portrait Gallery.

foreign jurisdiction; secondly, individual states of large area; and, thirdly, small scattered principalities which lie inside British districts or provinces. Of the first class, the Rajputana Agency, the Central Indian Agency, Baluchistan, and Kathiawar are the most important. Of the second class, Kashmir, Hyderabad, Mysore, and Baroda are the most conspicuous; but Travancore, Kolhapur, and Kutch may also be mentioned as considerable states. In the third class are included some hundreds of states, which vary in size from that of a district to a small collection of villages.

50. Groups of States.

Rājputana. The Rajputana Agency covers an area of 130,268 square miles, and is therefore larger than the whole of Bombay and Sindh. Its population of twelve millions is less than two-thirds of that of the Western Presidency. It includes twenty states, of which Tonk is Mahomedan, two are Jat, and the rest Rajput. In the extensive deserts of Rajputana the Rajputs, driven out of Hindustan by the Mahomedans, found a refuge for hundreds of years, and thus their chiefs of Mewar or Udaipur, Marwar or Jodhpur, and Jaipur, rank as the oldest princely families in India. Among the other states may be mentioned Bikanir, Jaisalmir, Bhartpur, Alwar, Kota, and Dholpur. They had suffered in turn from the exactions of the Delhi emperors, and from the incursions of the Pindaris and the Marathas, when in 1818 they were brought under the protection of the British. The chief political officer resides at Abu, and is styled the agent to the Governor-General.

Central India. The Central India Agency includes a larger number of states, which constitute a solid

MAIN GATE, GWALIOR.

block of 77,808 square miles in the very heart of India. Both in area and population it somewhat resembles the British province known as the Central Provinces. Gwalior is its chief state, and Indore the next in rank, but Bhopal, Rewa, and Ratlam also deserve special mention. The chief feature of this large group of principalities is its patchwork of territory and titles. Many petty estates nominally belonging to larger states are separately protected by the British government, and the possessions of the leading chiefs lie scattered about in small strips or patches, while some of the most important princes pay tribute to their inferiors. This result is due to the scrupulous fidelity of the British authorities to their engagements. When they intervened, the whole area was the scene of war and plunder. British armies suddenly proclaimed peace and order, and the conquerors, who prevented any further appeal to force and violence, undertook to secure all parties in possession of the rights and lands which they at that moment held. The chief political officer resides at Indore, from which centre he exercises control over Bundelkhand, Bhaghelkhand, Gwalior, Nimar, and Malwa.

Baluchistan. Baluchistan lies beyond the plains of the Indus, on the western frontier of India, and guards the approaches into Hindustan from Persia and Afghanistan. It consists of the territories of the Khan of Khelat and the Jam of Lus Beyla, and with the British province of Quetta falls under the political control of an officer of the government of India who resides at Quetta.

Kathiawar. The only other considerable block of several chiefships which needs notice is that of

Kathiawar, which is under the government of Bombay. Within an area of 20,559 square miles it affords the best possible study of the efforts made by the British to prevent native states "falling into the vortex of annexation." Under its treaty with the Peshwa the company might have introduced British rule into the province, but it preferred to make engagements with 147 chiefs, undertaking to protect them if they maintained order. About 80 of these estates in course of time were annexed to other chiefships, while the rest became split up under the local rules of succession into numerous petty estates. In 1863 the number of chiefships had risen to 418, and owing to disputes amongst the jurisdiction holders, and the frequency of boundary quarrels, robbery, and outlawry, it seemed as if annexation was inevitable. But this measure was avoided by dividing the larger chiefs into seven grades with different powers, by grouping the smaller ones round Thana circles, and by entrusting to political officers the trial of cases which the chiefs were unable to try. Thus Kathiawar remains under native rule, and the ordinary courts of justice established under British laws do not exercise authority in it.

51. Important Single States.

Hyderabad. The most extensive states in India under a single ruler are those which enjoy the fullest measure of internal authority. Some of them have already been mentioned above. Here we have to deal with a few of those which are not included in the groups of states already described. One of them, Hyderabad, with an area of 82,698 square miles, is nearly as large as the British province called the Central

Provinces. Its founder was a servant of the emperor of Delhi, who shook off the authority of his master when the Mahomedan power began to decline, and his successors have received considerable additions of territory from the British government as a reward for their military and political services.

Kashmir. Kashmir, which is almost of the same area as Hyderabad, was created by the British after the defeat of the Sikh army at the battle of Sobraon in 1846. The hill-country between the rivers Indus and Ravi, then acquired by conquest, was conferred upon Gulab Singh, Raja of Jammu, by the treaty of Amritzar.

Mysore. Mysore, a considerable state in the south of India, covering 28,000 square miles, rich in gold and fertile in soil, also owes its existence to British arms, by which it was restored to the Hindu dynasty from the hands of a usurper. Some years after this event, which occurred in 1799, the subjects of Mysore rose against the oppression and exactions of their Maharaja, and the British government took over the administration. On the death of the Maharaja in 1868 the British government again determined to revive the native rule, and they recognized his adopted son as his successor in 1881. His untimely death closed a career of great promise, and his son, a minor, succeeded him in 1894. Thus, after half a century of British administration, Mysore was once more placed under a native ruler, under certain conditions which afford a guarantee for the maintenance of the reforms introduced by the British commissioner.

Baroda. Baroda is another important state standing by itself in the fertile division of Guzerat in

Western India. Damaji, the founder of the line of Gaekwars, who rule this state of 8226 square miles, successfully maintained his position against the Marathas on the fall of the Mahomedan government in Ahmedabad. Baroda was thus formed into a native state many years after the establishment of British factories in Surat and Bombay, and at several periods in its history it has been sustained by British help. More recently, on the deposition of its ruler in 1875, who thus lost the benefit of the right of adoption granted to ruling chiefs, the British government allowed the widow of a former Gaekwar to adopt a member of the Gaekwar family who had been selected by the government of India as a suitable person upon whom to confer the state of Baroda.

There are many other states which stand out in the midst of British territory besides those described above. The honour of a salute, which varies from twenty-one guns to nine, indicates in a general way the degree of importance attached to a native chief. To the rulers of the three states of Baroda, Hyderabad, and Mysore the highest salute is given, and to the eight states of Bhopal, Gwalior, Indore, Kashmir, Khelat, Kolhapur, Mewar, and Travancore salutes of nineteen guns are given. Thirteen chiefs are entitled to seventeen guns, and seventeen receive a salute of fifteen guns. Besides these there are sixty-five other chiefs who are honoured with salutes. Judged then by this standard there are in India one hundred and six rulers of states who stand in the front rank. These figures, however, include several of the states which are massed together in groups like the Rajput and Central Indian states, as well as those which lie apart from others.

52. **Estates.** The third class of native states embraces many scattered portions of foreign territory lying in the midst of British districts. Such are the Jaghirs of Satara and the Southern Maratha country, the chiefships of the Central Provinces, and those of Orissa and others. It is not necessary to give a list of them, but any one who looks at the map of India will see at a glance that, if these states should prove bad neighbours or unable to maintain peace and order, they would only become thorns in the side of the local governments and district officers. A weak central government would have long ago given up as hopeless the task of controlling so many chiefships without the aid of British law and British courts. Their preservation is honourable to both parties. It testifies to the power of the suzerain government to protect the rights of the weak, and to the good sense of those chiefs who accept advice and co-operate with the British officers.

53. **Advantages of Native Rule.** The British government gains by the continuance of native rule several advantages. The states are a permanent object-lesson of the faithful adherence of the Indian authorities to their engagements. They also enable the people of India to compare the results of various systems of administration. Those who are curious to learn whether population, education, commerce, and industry increase more rapidly under one form of government than under another can answer this question for themselves. The British government at present contributes more to the states than they contribute to the welfare of British India. The cost of the naval and military defence of the empire, the upkeep of the ports and

dockyards, the main weight of expenditure on railways, and the expense of imperial establishments which benefit the whole of India, are borne almost entirely by the British provinces. The small payments which some states make under treaties more often represent a commutation charge for expenses of which they have been relieved than a contribution towards their share of protection from a foreign foe. But the princes and chiefs relieve the British government not merely of the cost of their local administration, but also of other civil responsibilities. So long as the chiefs are, in the words of Lord Canning's sanads, "loyal to the crown and faithful to the conditions of the treaties, grants, or engagements which record their obligations to the British government," they have nothing to fear from their powerful protector. All observers testify that under British advice great improvements have been effected in the administration of the states, and all friends of India look forward to the continuance of the union, and to the growth of a friendly rivalry between the officers of the Queen Empress and the princes of the states in promoting the prosperity of their respective subjects. The British have brought from the far west to the east new ideas of freedom and toleration. It may be hoped that in the best governed of the native states the new spirit will mix with the life of the Indian people, and that we shall learn from them what changes are best adapted to eastern habits.

"So let the change which comes be free
To ingroove itself with that which flies,
And work a joint of state, that plies
Its office, moved with sympathy."

CHAPTER VI.

THE SUPREME GOVERNMENT.

54. **National Concerns.** The reader has now gained a general idea of the frame-work of the Indian government. The empire consists of two parts, the native states and the British territories. The former are governed by their own rulers, who in certain matters follow the advice of the British government. The latter are divided into a number of villages and towns which are grouped into districts whose officers are the backbone of the executive government. The district officers obey the local government, and it is the local government or administration which rules over the province. But just as we have seen that the affairs of the province are conducted partly by local or municipal boards and partly by the officers of the provincial government, so in the larger area of British India there are some matters which lie within the sphere of the authority of the provincial governor, and others of a national character which are reserved for the orders of the central government of India. In order that there may be no confusion or conflict of authority, it is necessary that each local government

should recognize and obey one and the same supreme power, and that the government of India should in its turn avoid interference in the affairs which belong to the provinces. Upon a good understanding between the central and provincial governments the smooth working of the whole machine mainly depends. It was for the lack of such an agreement and unity of purpose that the great empire bequeathed by Akbar to his successors fell to pieces. The viceroys and local governors appointed to rule over the provinces rebelled against the central authority at Delhi, and their disobedience broke up the whole frame of the Mahomedan government.

55. **Supreme Control.** No one therefore who knows his history will value lightly the need for a good understanding between the local governments which command the civil officers of India, and the imperial government which gives directions to the governors and heads of administration. The first step towards such an agreement is to realize the necessity for one supreme control. It is wanted for three purposes—to adjust differences between the local governments; to represent all of them in external concerns—that is to say, affairs affecting foreign governments; and thirdly, to give uniformity to the actions of several separate authorities which are working within their own provinces.

It is not difficult to see that the interests of one province may be opposed to those of another, and that to avoid a conflict a third party must intervene and settle the dispute. One province enjoys access to the highway of commerce—the sea—and if it were left to itself, it might enrich itself by taxing goods in transit to or from the ports of the empire. Another province lies on the frontier exposed to the attacks of hostile tribes, and the cost of its military defence is very heavy. But since its military operations protect not only its own districts, but the provinces which lie behind it, its government has a just claim to recover from the rest of the empire some part of its military expenditure. A third province is exposed to an irregular monsoon, and frequently suffers famine when its neighbour enjoys good crops and high prices for its surplus. In these and many other cases that might be mentioned a court of appeal is needed to decide what contributions one province should make to another.

Take now a different case where it is proposed to make a treaty of commerce or a political arrangement with another nation. The effect of such a treaty upon the whole of India must be considered, and the interests of one local government may be opposed to those of another. The foreign power can only deal with India as a whole, and it must look to one supreme authority to speak in the name of the empire and to compel all parts of it to abide by the agreement arrived at.

Again, in the internal administration of the country it is essential that progress should be made on certain uniform lines. It may be necessary that the systems of education followed in each province should be examined by a Commission, and the operations of the various local departments brought into harmony with a general plan. In all these matters the local governments, with their knowledge limited to their own districts, are not in a position to form an independent judgment. A supreme authority, without prejudice or preference for a particular locality, is better able to deal with matters which are national rather than provincial concerns.

56. **The Government of India.** Accordingly, besides the local governments, there is a body known as the Government of India. It consists of a viceroy and governor-general, who is sent out from England to preside over it for a period of five years. He is assisted by a council composed of the commander-in-chief in India; a councillor versed in law, who has charge of the legislative department; another who takes the financial department; and three other members who preside over the home and revenue departments, the public works, and the military department. There are large offices under secretaries for each of the six departments mentioned above, to which must be added the foreign department, of which the viceroy usually takes charge. Just as the local governments have councils for making laws and regulations, so the viceroy has a similar council, of which his colleagues in the executive government are members. Such is the constitution of the central government, and we must now see where it resides, what duties it discharges, and by what authority and force it is controlled.

57. **Provincial Capitals.** The question of the best residence for the government of India has given rise to much discussion. In order to form a correct judgment, it is necessary to dismiss from the mind false notions based on a consideration of the places chosen as the seats of provincial governments. The duties of local governments and of the central government are quite distinct. The former administer affairs, while

GOVERNMENT HOUSE, CALCUTTA.

the latter controls their administration from above. Their choice of residence must in each case depend upon these varying conditions. Let us then see where the local governments are placed. It will be remembered that the Emperor Akbar called his subahs or provinces by the names of the chief city within them, and the British government, in the cases of Madras and Bombay, has adopted the same plan. But in the majority of the provinces, some geographical or racial distinction has suggested a title in preference to that of a city. There are perhaps two reasons for this change. Under Moghal rule no pains and expense were spared to give honour and dignity to the city in which the provincial viceroy of the empire resided. The British government, on the other hand, spends its public revenues on the improvement of roads and railways, and on projects of irrigation and other works, which will benefit not the city only but the province. Another reason for the avoidance of a local title in the description of a political or administrative division of the empire is afforded by the tendency of cities to rise or fall. The most famous cities of the past, such as Bijapur, Vijianagar, Ujjain, have long since lost their pre-eminence, whilst others more favourably situated for commerce, trade, or defence have taken the lead from them. These in turn may lose their position. But although in the British divisions of India special cities have ceased to give their names to the provinces, there is in every local government or administration one city recognized as its centre or capital, where the local government resides in close contact with the life and feelings of the population. In these cities or towns are established the chief courts of law, the provincial offices of government, and the houses of firms and merchants carrying on the trades, industries, and commerce upon which the province depends. They are the head-quarters or the capitals of the province, the centre of its multiform activity and public life, chosen in order that the governing and governed classes may be in close touch with each other.

58. **Simla.** On the other hand, a supreme government charged with such national concerns as those already described does not need to be established in a capital city like the governments of the provinces. The provincial governor is the head of the executive officers and the recognized advocate and guardian of local interests. He must be in personal relations with his district officers on the one hand, and with the best representatives of provincial opinion on the other. But the government of India, charged with large powers of control and supervision, and called upon to decide between the conflicting interests of provinces should, it is thought, detach itself from such influences as are local and special, and whilst keeping itself informed as to the opinion of all parts of the empire, it should hold the balance impartially. For this reason it has been considered desirable that the supreme government should not reside for the whole year in Calcutta, but should spend a portion of it in the north on the slopes of the Himalayas, where the climate is favourable for prolonged work in office, and whence the affairs not merely of one province but of all provinces can be watched. There are some who think that the supreme government when it descends into the plains should not invariably go to one and the same city, Calcutta, but should visit in turn the several

EUROPEAN HOUSES, SIMLA.

provinces and thus, in course of years, come into equal contact with them all. The only objection to this plan would be the cost of buildings and the heavy expense involved in moving the records of the Imperial offices. Perhaps the present arrangement is on the whole the most economical and advantageous, when the duties devolving upon the government of India are considered.

59. **Imperial Duties.** The functions of the supreme government may be described as either original or appellate. In some matters it takes the lead and directs action, while in other matters it corrects the action taken by the local governments and administrations. Its original jurisdiction is exercised in the following concerns:

i. Foreign relations, including war, treaties, and consular arrangements,
ii. Measures affecting the army and marine forces,
iii. Imperial legislation,
iv. General taxation,
v. Matters of currency and debt,
vi. The post office, telegraphs, and railroads,
vii. Emigration,
viii. Mineral resources.

Its appellate jurisdiction covers the whole area of the administration, legislation, and expenditure of the local governments. Parties or bodies who are aggrieved by the action of the provincial authorities can seek redress from the government of India by presenting appeals in accordance with the petition rules published for general guidance. But quite apart from such appeals, the Governor-General in Council has, under the authority of an Act of Parliament, a general power to superintend, control, and direct the several governments in all points relating to the civil or military government of their territories. In particular, certain functions are expressly reserved by parliament and by the various legislatures of India for exercise by the supreme government, so that the same law which gives to local authorities power to act, requires that in certain directions they should only use their legal powers if the supreme government approves.

60. **Wide Range of Imperial Action.** Complaints are sometimes heard that too much authority is exercised by the Government of India, and that the executive officers in the provinces or districts are weakened thereby. Those who feel this danger must bear in mind the reasons which have suggested the distribution of work just described. The frontiers of India extend from Arabia to the river Mekong, and even touch Abyssinia on the Somali coast of Africa. Some great powers of the west—Russia, France, and Turkey—hold territories that are in contact with India or its protected states. The empires of China, Persia, and Afghanistan are its close neighbours. The conduct of British and Indian relations with these powers and states is a difficult matter, frequently touching on dangerous ground. It must rest with one supreme authority in India to hold in its hands all the strings of foreign policy. Equally necessary is it that the power which dictates the policy should be able to execute it, and should command all the resources and means of offence and defence. The military and naval forces of India may have to work together, and in time of peace, arms, equipments, and all the machinery of war must be prepared and maintained with an eye to uniformity. Delay and confusion on the eve of war

can only be prevented by the issue of orders from a central authority.

Similar considerations apply also to legislation and taxation. There is not a law passed by any provincial legislature which the council of the Governor-General for making laws could not pass. But its legislative action is reserved for those matters which require to be dealt with at the centre of the empire. Laws affecting the finances, or those which apply to every province in India, like the procedure codes or jail acts, and in some cases laws which involve new principles of an experimental character, like the Dekhan relief act, are passed by the imperial legislature, which also legislates for provinces having no law-making councils of their own. Since the whole machinery of government depends upon the proceeds of taxation, the supreme government takes charge of the ways and means. It provides the legal powers for taxing the empire, and it assigns to the several provinces their share of the proceeds. It prepares the budget and feels the pulse of the accounts from month to month, so as to contract expenditure if need be, and thus ensure the solvency of the empire. No debt can be incurred by any local or provincial authority without its sanction, and the difficult subject of currency is dealt with by it. Imperial departments like the post office, the telegraph, and the railway, which carry on their operations in every part of India, are directly administered by it in the interests of public economy and safety. Finally, it acts for each province in all cases where action must be based upon information and statistics collected throughout the empire, in which case the local governments could not obtain from district officers not subject to them the requisite data for themselves. Therefore the supreme government watches the course of trade, collects from stations inside and outside of India observations and returns of wind, tide, and rainfall, and fixes the terms upon which the mineral resources of the country are to be prospected or worked. In short, the business of India, like that of any large mercantile firm, is partly conducted at the head-quarters, and partly at the branches, and matters of principle, or those which concern all the branches, are decided by the central authority.

61. **Provincial Contracts.** In the list of imperial duties given above there is one headed "general taxation," upon which it is necessary to make some remarks. If it were left to the thirteen provinces to supply themselves with funds by imposing such taxes as they thought fit, there would inevitably be inequality and ground for complaint. The supreme government therefore settles what taxes shall be imposed, and it divides amongst the provinces the funds so collected, reserving for itself the means for discharging its own duties. Before Lord Mayo entered on his term of office as viceroy, the local governments annually received such provision for the purpose of their administration as the government of India chose to allot, and if they wanted additional funds they asked for them. Whether they got what they wanted or not, depended upon the state of the finances and the claims or good fortune of other applicants. The local governments collected the taxes and revenues for the supreme government, and had no personal interest in expanding them. So long as their own demands were satisfied

they had no particular motive for economy. Lord Mayo devised a new system which his successors have improved. Under present arrangements a contract is made for a term of years with the local governments. To them are allotted certain shares in the land-revenue and in the receipts from forests, stamps, excise, assessed taxes, and other sources of income. They have thus a direct interest in the collection of these taxes and revenues, and the imperial treasury, which receives its share, benefits by their success. At the same time they are made responsible for the whole, or a fixed proportion, of the expenditure upon certain departments, so that they also benefit by economy. They are by these means encouraged to make the most of the revenues of their province, and to reduce as much as possible the cost of collection and administration, because they profit by their own vigilance and economy. What they gain or save they can then spend on public works, or other public demands that will benefit the population of their own provinces. They are entrusted with certain funds, and they may make them go as far as they can according to their own discretion. The supreme government is relieved from the difficulty of deciding between rival claims for additional means advanced by several provinces, when once it has fixed the contract. It can easily be understood that in settling the grants fairly for all the provinces an impartial judge is needed, and for this purpose a supreme government is indispensable.

62. **Departments.** It is sometimes said that the government of India is a government by departments, and hence it is called a bureaucratic government. It

is obvious that the great machine of administration must be moved by several wheels, each performing its own separate duties, although all are set in motion by the same motive power acting upon one principal wheel. In every large business there must be a division of labour, because skill and experience are gained by entrusting the several parts of it to different sets of men, who thus become familiar with all the details of their particular branch of the trade or business. In a native state the hand of the chief minister is felt in every department. He makes the law and he executes it. Whatever is done in any part of the state springs from his, or his master's, personal will. But in British India, where the government consists of a governor-general in council, or a governor in council, the charge of the departments is divided amongst the members of council, great questions in each department being reserved for discussion and decision by the whole body. Where the province is under a lieutenant-governor, or a chief commissioner, there is no board of council to refer to, but the advice of the secretaries in the department concerned is at the command of the head of the province. In each province of the empire business falls into the same departments as those which are recognized by the supreme government, although it may be necessary for the sake of economy to place two or more of them under the same secretary. The secretariat of the government of India is divided into seven departments. The military department includes also the marine. The financial deals not only with the finances, but also with the post-office and telegraph, with opium, customs, and salt revenue, currency and mints, and trade and commerce. The foreign department deals with the relations of India with foreign powers, and with the native states of the empire; and the corresponding department under local governments is called the political. The legislative department deals with projects of law and rules made under Acts, and also advises the other departments on legal matters. The home department has a wide range of concerns, including education, medical and sanitary measures, judicial and ecclesiastical affairs, police, jails, and municipal government. The revenue department has charge of revenue and scientific surveys, settlements, forests, patents of invention, emigration, meteorological forecasts, museums and exhibitions, and when necessary it controls the administration of famine relief. The public works department deals with roads, buildings, railways, and irrigation. This short account of the manifold duties of the Indian government will serve to show how necessary it is to entrust them to separate departments. We have next to consider the means by which the supreme government in India is controlled by an authority at the very centre of the British empire.

63. **Secretary of State for India.** The government of India, although it is supreme in India, is nevertheless subject to a large measure of control from without. In 1858 the Parliament of Great Britain and Ireland passed an Act for the better government of India, and transferred to one of Her Majesty's principal secretaries of state the powers of the East India Company and of the court of directors. A council was created to assist him in the discharge

of his duties. In regard to appointments and patronage, contracts and property, the Secretary of State in Council was invested with precise authority; and it was laid down that the expenditure of the revenues of India, both in India and elsewhere, should be subject to his control. The supreme power of the purse thus vests in the cabinet minister, who presides over his council at the India Office in London. By him a statement of Indian finances is annually presented to Parliament, and a further statement is prepared from detailed reports so as to exhibit the moral and material progress and condition of India in every province of it. Thus the whole administration passes under his review. Again, if any order is sent to India directing the actual commencement of hostilities by Her Majesty's forces in India, the fact of such order having been sent must be communicated to Parliament; and except for preventing or repelling actual invasion of Her Majesty's Indian possessions, the revenues of India cannot, without the consent of both Houses of Parliament, be applied to military operations carried on beyond the external frontiers of such possessions. Every law or regulation passed by the Indian councils, and approved by the Viceroy, must be reported to the Secretary of State, and the Sovereign may signify Her disallowance of it through the Secretary of State in Council. These important powers by no means exhaust Her authority or the authority of the Secretary of State in Council. He can give orders to every officer in India, including the Governor-General, and he may dismiss from the service any servant of government. He advises the Queen Empress as to the appointment of the Viceroy, the Governors of Madras and Bombay, the members of their councils, the judges of the high court, and certain other high officers. The Secretary of State in Council may make rules as to the distribution of patronage, and, with the advice of the Civil Service Commissioners, as to the admission of candidates to the civil service. It is unnecessary here to enter into greater detail as to the powers of the Secretary of State: but it must be observed that he is a member of the Cabinet which governs the United Kingdom, and the Cabinet is responsible to Parliament for its conduct in India, as well as in the other parts of the Queen's territories and dominions. All the checks, then, which the constitution of the United Kingdom, its public opinion, and its press supply, operate upon the administration of India, and afford effective safe-guards against any misuse by the Indian authorities of the powers entrusted to them.

CHAPTER VII.

THE POPULATION OF INDIA.

64. **Diversities of Race.** The strength of a whole country, like that of any single citizen of it, depends upon the variety and qualities of its several members. Man's position in the created world is the result of his excellent powers of brain and limbs severally suited for his advancement and self-defence. So too the most prosperous nations are those which can make the best use of the resources which nature has placed at their command. History shows that different races of mankind possess special qualities and aptitudes. Some excel in fighting whether by land or sea, others are skilled in the arts of peace, some prefer agriculture or commerce, while others are famed as artizans or miners. The most prosperous community is that which contains a complete assortment of all useful conditions of men. The country of India enjoys great natural advantages of climate, scenery, and position. Protected on three sides by the ocean, it is guarded on the north by mountain barriers of high elevation. Its highlands, plains, and lowlands present a great variety of climates and of the earth's products.

Many of its rivers are capable of navigation, and its forests are rich in timber. Its mineral wealth in gold and coal is considerable. It is true that a great part of the land is liable to scarcity when the yearly rains are withheld owing to causes over which the best of governments can have no control. But in the rivers which carry down the melted snow from the Himalayas to the plains, and in several excellent sites for storing large supplies of water, it possesses some compensation for this physical disadvantage, and the physical conditions of the provinces are so various that a general loss of crops throughout the whole of India has never been known. Its population of 287 millions is a numerical force which under judicious management ought to provide the country with all that it can require. The main essentials are the power to defend its natural frontiers by land and sea, the maintenance of internal peace, the development of its trade and commerce, and a good administration. For promoting these objects its various classes of population are admirably adapted, and notwithstanding obvious differences of race and religion there is no section of the population which does not contribute to the good of others and advance the general welfare. In this chapter some account will be given of the chief races to whom it may be said that "God has lent you India for your life; it is a great entail"; a land which was long ago called the *Bharata Varcha* or the fertile land, or again the land of the *Jambu Dvipa*, the fruitful myrtle that kisses heaven. But every country is after all that which its inhabitants make it, and India has passed through many changes of fortune and much distress.

65. **The Hindus.** The Hindus deserve the first place in any account of the population, not merely by reason of their numbers, nearly 208 millions, but because they were the first to bring social order and religious discipline to the country. The mind loses itself in the mists of six thousand years ago, when it attempts to follow the colonies of the Sanskrit-speaking Aryans, as they slowly drove their flocks and herds through the rocky gorges cut out by the Indus into the land of the Punjab. We know however that, as they advanced, the aboriginal races fell back into the refuge of the forests and into the solitude of the mountains, where their descendants still reside, avoiding contact with the people of the plains. The Aryans established themselves in Bharma Varta, the country lying between the Sarasvati (now called the Sarsuti) and the Dreshadvati, a stream near Thanesar. From this cradle they extended their rule throughout India. In course of time other invaders—Scythians, Pahlavas, and Yavanas—followed their tracks, but they all in turn found their places in the Hindu system alongside of the conquered Dasyus; and thus was established social order in India upon that basis of caste which Hindu society has maintained for so many centuries. The services rendered to India by the Aryans are to this day enjoyed by their descendants, and the sacred books of the East edited by Max Müller, Menu's Code, the languages of India, and numerous records in stone and marble bear witness to the work which they accomplished in changing the half civilized races of India into a society of orderly citizens. Their power of conversion, inherited by their descendants, has been

exercised in modern times over the Kakhyins of Mongoloid stock in Manipur, over the chiefs of Tipperah, in Nepal, and in other places where the outer ranks of Hindu society gain recruits from the population which surrounds it. To the Aryans and their Hindu followers the empire of India owes its first lessons in civilization, in agriculture, and in the arts of peace and settled government.

66. **Mahomedans.** The victories of peace are not however the only victories which a nation must win in order to preserve its own. India learnt this lesson to her cost, when her fair cities in the north were sacked by fanatical invaders from the mountainous country on the north-west, and the peaceful inhabitants given over to the sword. The very blessings which Aryan rule had conferred upon Hindustan sorely tempted the greed of the Pathan soldier, and the Hindus found themselves quite powerless to hurl back the Mahomedan invader from the Indus. In the eighth century of the Christian era Sindh fell a prey to the conqueror, and in 977 A.D. another of the gates of India, Peshawar, was opened and held by the Ghaznevites. The holy temple of Somnath was plundered in 1024, and ill-fated Delhi lay at the mercy of the men of Ghaz in 1193. India offered to its hardy invaders not merely spoil but a home, and by the 13th century the Mahomedans, thenceforward entitled to regard themselves as citizens of the Indian Empire, began to adorn their new country with the graceful colonnade of the Kutab Minar and other noble buildings. Their wave of conquest spread to the south, and in 1347 the Bahmani dynasty, mother of the five Mahomedan states of Ahmednagar,

Bijapur, Golkonda, Ellichpur, and Bidar, had risen to power.

THE KUTAB MINAR AT DELHI.

Soon afterwards the country was again reminded that its north-western frontier was for ever exposed to foreign invasion, and that the people of India could only maintain their liberties by constant proof of military power. Where the Hindus had failed the Mahomedans also proved to be insufficient, when the storm of Tamerlane burst on the north in 1398. Akbar, by his great abilities, once more restored peace and order throughout the empire, and it seemed as if at length a settled government had been established in the land. But again a Persian invader, Nadir Shah, poured his armies into the northern provinces in 1739, and it was discovered that Aryan civilization, even with the Mahomedan additions to the fighting strength of India, was of no avail in any struggle with the fresh strong blood of invading armies, recruited in colder climates and constantly exercised in the profession of arms. Something more was needed to insure peace to the country, and to protect the lives and properties of its population from the assaults of its neighbours. But the events which we have briefly noticed at least added an important element of strength to the Indian population; for, although the Hindus still outnumber all other classes of the community, the Mahomedans contribute more than 57 millions to the defence and support of the empire.

67. **The Parsis.** From what quarter of the globe the India of to-day has drawn the means of military and naval defence, necessary for her safety and advancement, will be presently shown. But before that account is given, we must notice a small but highly useful contribution to the empire, which is supplied by the addition of 90,000 Parsis. The Hindus organized a system of trade in their arrangement of castes, but it was rather an internal, or

a local, trade which they provided. A spirit of enterprise which crosses seas to find markets, and establishes commerce with foreign countries on a large scale, was wholly alien to Hindu feelings. Nor were the Mahomedans, who brought their swords to India, well fitted to supply the need. Their experiences were not of peaceful commerce, but rather of war and its rougher methods; yet history has proved that no country can prosper which does not carry on intercourse with other countries, and exchange its products for foreign goods. Nature has distributed over the world her various gifts, and the value of what one country possesses is determined by the wants of others. The timber which would have rotted in Indian forests has served to build the ships of countries separated by many thousands of miles from the shores of India, whilst in recent years the Indian people have bought their articles of dress more cheaply from the west than they could manufacture them at home. For iron and steel, so necessary to the people's comfort, she has hitherto depended mainly on foreign countries. A spirit of enterprise which follows trade into distant lands is a special gift which Providence has conferred upon particular classes of men. The persecuted fugitives from Khorassan, who fled from the bloody field of Nahavand, found in the eighth century of the Christian era a place of refuge on the coast of Daman in Western India. In the fifteenth century their descendants had formed colonies in Naosari, Cambay, Surat, and Thana, and to-day the Parsis constitute the backbone of Indian commercial enterprise. There is not an advanced outpost of the empire, in Arabia, on the Somali coast of Africa, in

Baluchistan, or even in the far off Shan states of Burma, which is not occupied by some of them. In wealth and education they occupy a foremost position in the Indian population, and in enriching themselves they benefit the cultivators and artizans of India, whose products they sell, by opening up new markets for their industries.

68. **Aborigines.** The aborigines present a great variety of speech, race, and colour. The fair skinned Panikas of Chutia Nagpur side by side with the negro-looking Lohars, the black Garos, the dark-skinned Kols, the Madras Puliyars, the kilted Nagas, the wild head-hunting Was of Burma, and the better known Santhals, Kondhs, Gonds, Maris, and Bhils, seem to defy all attempts to treat such varied classes of aborigines as coming from a common stock. Conquest or policy may have settled by force these different colonies of men in remote parts of the empire, just as the Kafirs of Kafiristan have of late been transplanted into Afghanistan from their own country. Science has endeavoured by examination of their skulls, by observation of their colour, and even by a comparison of their languages, to pierce the darkness of history, and to establish theories as to their past. The only facts regarding them which concern us here are that they are estimated at more than nine millions, that they are in a very backward state of education and civilization, that they are capable of great endurance and possessed of keen faculties, and that they offer to the more advanced communities a field for sympathy and influence.

69. **Other Sections.** In estimating the capacity

of the Indian people to turn to the best account what nature has placed at their disposal, one must not omit a brief notice of some other sections of the population. The Buddhists of India, excluded in the census from the returns of the Hindu religion, number seven millions, and they are chiefly found in Burma. In this frontier province India is gradually admitting into her civil ranks the skilled artizan and the patient labourer of Chinese origin. The empire's power of producing wealth is thus strengthened and enlarged. The Sikhs at the other extremity of the country, although they number only two millions, have won for themselves an enduring reputation as soldiers, and they have upheld the interests of India upon many a field of battle.

70. **The Europeans.** It has been shown that India is a large country, rich in natural resources, possessing a huge population capable of supplying all forms of labour, and claiming as her sons many races of men. The qualities of these various races are diverse, but united they ought to render the empire safe against attack, and be able to produce those results in all fields of man's activity which sum up so much of human happiness. The course of Indian history shows, however, in the clearest light three serious dangers to which the lives and properties of the people of India were constantly exposed up to the end of the eighteenth century. Those dangers were liability to attack by sea, physical deterioration of the military forces, and isolation.

Even at the strongest period of Mahomedan rule India could not keep a naval enemy from her coasts, or protect her navigable rivers from the attacks of pirates.

The kings of Bijapur and the emperors of Delhi sought to supply this deficiency by employing Africans, and the Sidhi admirals of the fleet were given Jaghirs as a condition of defending India by sea. This means of naval defence broke down, and one nation after another crossed the seas from Europe and settled upon the coasts of India. The rivers were infested with pirates whom the civil governments failed to suppress. In the British settlers whom the Indian chiefs invited to establish factories, the country has at last found the sea-power which is able to supply a want that the ranks of Indian society could not fill.

The admission of the British into the life of India not only relieved it of the difficulty it experienced on sea, but solved a further problem in its defence by land. It has been seen that, when the Mahomedan invaders from the north-west settled down to peaceful lives in India, the influence of the climate and the change of life weakened their military strength. The children of warriors proved, after many years of rest and exposure to the heat of the Indian plains, unable to repel fresh invaders from beyond the mountains. The British army, which under British rule India now employs in her service, comes and goes, and it is constantly renewed from the original source of supply. Thus the merchants whom the emperor of Delhi invited to trade have brought with them a valuable contribution to the military resources of the empire.

Hardly less important is the third boon conferred by the British on the Indian people. Cut off by the mountains from contact with other countries, Hindustan was practically excluded from the blessings which discovery and science have bestowed on Western nations. The railway, the telegraph, the manufactory, and the mining industry, were the first fruits of Indian contact with Europe, a contact which has to be maintained across thousands of miles of sea.

The Europeans who have in the last century taken their place amongst the population of India are numerically very few. Their strength lies in the fact that, whatever may be their duties, whether as civil servants of the state, as soldiers, or as merchants and pioneers of industries, they are drawn fresh from the fountain head of British power. As they fall out of the ranks their places are taken by others, and deterioration is prevented by the fact that the supply is constantly renewed.

71. **Jarring Concord.** The Indian people are a collection of various races, various religions, and numerous speeches. Their ways of life and thought are different, and it is often the fashion to dwell on their jarring interests. But in the first chapter of this book it was shown that the body politic, or the nation, consists, like the human body, of several members; and if the finger is hurt, the whole man feels the pain. The special qualities and possessions of each class of the Indian population are the possession of the whole empire. Perfect union and common action for the moral and material progress of India can exist side by side with separate interests. Nay, even the assertion by one class of its rights permitted by law tends to create a wider respect for the rights of others and mutual toleration. This

thought is well expressed by the poet Pope in these verses:

"The less the greater, set so justly true
That touching one must strike the other too;
Till jarring interests of themselves create
The according music of a well mix'd state.
Such is the world's great harmony that springs
From order, union, full consent of things,
More powerful each as needful to the rest,
And in proportion as it blesses, blest."

CHAPTER VIII.

THE TRADES AND OCCUPATIONS OF INDIA.

72. **Division of Labour.** The masses of the people in all countries maintain themselves by means of their own labour, and from the proceeds of their occupations taxes also are paid and the administration carried on. Nothing, therefore, is of greater consequence to the people and to the government than a steady supply of work for the population. The nation's working hands should be employed upon several trades and industries, and the people ought to be free to choose the form of labour, which from time to time may be the most profitable. If, for instance, Indian workmen relied wholly upon agricultural work, their hands would be idle whenever it pleased Providence to withhold the rains, or if the crops should be destroyed by locusts or other visitations. It is therefore important that India should have other resources besides the cultivation of its soil. Again, if labour is misapplied, there can only be waste and poverty. Labourers must be ready to adapt themselves to changes of circumstances. The trade of the Brinjarns, or carriers of goods on pack saddles, ceased to be required or profitable when good

roads were made and carts introduced. A greater change occurred when railways were made. People who want to fetch goods from a distance, or to send them to market, will not pay heavy charges for an expensive mode of transit, when they can save expense by using carts or railways. All classes of men must benefit by improved communications, and even the old order of carriers and cartmen are sure to find new labour in some more profitable occupation. There is thus a constant division and change of occupation in a prosperous community. For this reason experience proves that a government is unwise if it makes laws or rules which interfere with the absolute freedom of industry and trade. Provided that it sees that employers of labour do not expose their men to danger of life or limb, the State may safely leave the rest to the parties themselves. If one trade decays and another thrives, the people are the first to discover and feel the change; and as each man knows for himself, far better than government can do, the sort of labour which suits him, he should be left free to follow his own interests in the choice of work.

73. **Capital.** There is, however, something which a government can do in order to help people to find labour. It can, by maintaining peace and justice, encourage others to give an impulse to labour, and to set in motion the activities of artizans and labourers. That impulse can alone be given by capital. When in old times the people of Mysore collected gold from the Kolar fields, they carried their pickings straight to the goldsmiths or traders, who paid them on the spot for their labour. But a time came when the gold lay concealed in the depths of the earth, and when expen-

sive machinery was needed to extract it, and to bring it up to a place where stamping machines and human hands could deal with it. There was no man of means in the country who was prepared to spend his money on a mere chance that he would be repaid one day by a profitable business. So the Mysore gold mines were deserted, and the miners lost their livelihood, until lately some Englishmen in a far off country across the seas subscribed their money and sent to Mysore the required machinery. There are many other industries in cotton, tea, coffee, cinchona, indigo, jute, iron, coal, paper, and silk, which have in the same way been opened to Indian labour by the aid of foreign capital. A country may possess large natural resources, and an abundant supply of labourers, but without capital it cannot take advantage of its possessions. For this reason, the "Bombay Presidency Association," in preparing an address to the Queen-Empress Victoria on the completion of sixty years of her reign, laid particular stress upon the influx of British capital as one of the greatest benefits received by India. They wrote as follows:

"In all these various ways the peace and prosperity of the country have been promoted, with the result that during the past sixty years the population has multiplied nearly 100 per cent. cultivation has extended so as to keep pace with this growth, and trade and commerce have flourished beyond all previous measure, and been beneficial both to England and India. India has become the chief customer of British manufacture and trade, and it affords a safe investment for the employment of nearly 500 millions of British capital in the development of Indian agriculture, manufacture, and trade. The bonds which unite the two countries have thus become indissoluble, and under British protection the various races of India, speaking different languages and professing different creeds, have learnt to feel for the first time that the connection between the two countries is a providential arrangement intended to weld them altogether into a great Indian nation, owning common allegiance to the same sovereign and having common interests in the promotion of peace and good-will throughout the land."

74. **Occupations.** According to the last census out of 287 millions nearly 172 millions were supported by agriculture, and more than 25 millions by general labour including earthwork. More than 12½ millions of people, including their families, were engaged in providing textile fabrics and dress, and nearly 4 millions in working up metals and stones. On the other hand the persons, including all the members of their families, who were supported by the public service, or employed in the service of self-government boards and of native states, numbered only 5,600,153 Thus it appears that agriculture is the mainstay of Indian labour. In reality it supported a far larger number than 172 millions, because those employed in the care of cattle, the preparation of food-stuffs, and the construction of carts, indirectly live on the cultivation of the soil. The great difference between India and Great Britain lies in this, that the mass of the people of India depend on the country's crops and, therefore, on the seasons, whilst the British not only import their food, but also the raw material of their industries, and work it up for the market. India thus sends her cotton, her indigo, and her

timber to England, where the skilled labour of the British artizan is employed upon adapting the produce of foreign soils to the use of mankind. Since a great part of India is subjected to risk of drought, locusts, and other influences hostile to agriculture, it has always been the policy of the British government to open out to its labouring population new sources of industry and wealth, thus relieving the pressure on the soil and enabling the working classes to pursue their occupations, although the crops may for a season be withered owing to a want of rain.

75. **Mines.** We may examine a few of the methods by which this desirable end has been promoted. India possesses beneath the soil many of those mineral resources which have made England rich and industrious. But before the establishment of British rule there was no enterprise or capital available for meeting the heavy expenses of setting up the required machinery; and, moreover, there was no experience or skilled labour in India capable of working the mines. Until quite lately India imported from England, or from Australia or Japan, all the coal required for her railways or factories. She is now able to supply from the Bengal coal mines, the Singareni field, and other sources, 3,537,000 tons of coal annually, and in this single industry 50,000 workmen are employed in a labour which neither famine nor drought need interrupt. To these 50,000 must be added the families they support, and one must remember the many other occupations which the transport of, and the trade in, coal support. There is a splendid future in store for the Indian coal, which is not only well able to supply all the growing demands of the country,

but is sure to find in other countries of Asia a rich market. Besides this the coal trade is itself the parent of other trades.

For India possesses plenty of iron, and with cheap coal it may be able to produce steel and iron for its railways, its factories, and its buildings. The gold mines of Mysore have shown what capital and European skill can do for the country. They are giving an annual output of 305,000 ounces of pure gold, extracted from workings which Indian industry, left to itself, was obliged to abandon as being no longer able to pay the cost of labour. The Mysore government, without spending a rupee upon the works, derives from them a royalty of nearly ten lakhs a year, besides an immense addition to its excise and other revenue, while an army of native workmen paid for by the English companies supports itself in comfort by means of the gold-mining industry.

76. **Tea and Coffee.** Capital and labour are the most important elements of wealth and production. But they are not everything. Hardly less essential are the skill and experience which discover the road to new industries. When the first English settlers arrived in Bombay, they found it a sandy waste. Within a few years they had brought the Persian rose and other shrubs and flowers from neighbouring countries, and had adorned the settlement with the beautiful mass of foliage and flowers for which it has since been famed amongst the cities of the East. Their example has been followed by their successors. In 1820 some European planters settled in Mysore, and in the Wynaad, and they set to work to convert these hilly jungle-tracts into coffee

gardens. There are now in the south of India 310,500 acres of land, otherwise useless, brought under coffee and tea cultivation. Their exports of coffee, tea, and cinchona are valued at 277 lakhs of rupees. They employ altogether some 323,000 workmen and overseers, who receive 187 lakhs of rupees in wages. In addition the carriers of the produce, and the traders engaged in its sale, employ many other persons.

TEA-TREE. LEAVES AND FLOWERS OF TEA-TREE.

In 1835 some far-seeing Europeans sent to the south of India boxes of plants of tea raised from Chinese seed, and in 1859 a similar experiment was made with cinchona. These products have not proved quite so successful in Madras and Mysore as coffee has, but in Assam the tea industry gives employment to 500,000 natives, and the value of the crop exported is 500 lakhs of rupees. In many other parts of India the cultivation of tea is adding to the wealth of the country, and the labourers engaged in it are reckoned at 440,000 permanently employed, and 156,000 temporarily employed. No less than 415,000 acres in India are covered with tea plantations.

77. **Cotton.** But the most striking of all the benefits which British capital and British experience have conferred upon the labour of India is the establishment of the cotton industry. England for a long period possessed almost a monopoly of this branch of trade, but her fellow-citizens of the East have now learnt from her how to use their own natural resources so as to compete with Great Britain in supplying not only Indian but other Asiatic countries with cotton goods. At the beginning of the nineteenth century, beyond its agricultural produce, India had few products, except Dacca muslins, dyes, and pottery, which were valued by foreign nations. It has now of late years taken rank as a manufacturing country. It can boast of some 147 cotton-mills worked by steam, which employ 150,000 hands; so rapidly has this single industry grown since the first mill was introduced by the British in 1851. Besides these it has 29 jute-mills, giving work to 79,000 hands, and 71 rice-cleaning mills, 68 saw-mills and 8 paper-factories, which between them employ 49,000 workmen, besides 63 tanneries, 51 iron-foundries, 54 flour-mills, 56 oil factories, and 41 tobacco-factories, employing many thousands of labourers. An impulse is being given to the silk industry, and there is no direction in which British enterprise and capital are not pushing their way in order to extend the manufactures of India, and thus to open up to its vast population new trades and industries. The trade returns of Indian commerce, as well as the census figures of "occupations or means of subsistence," show plainly the magnitude of the revolu-

tion in the industrial life of India which is taking place. All this activity means new sources of income to the working-men of India and profitable openings for its tradesmen and capitalists. The fact is too easily forgotten that for centuries the country has had at its command coal, gold, petroleum, tea, coffee, and cotton, and yet it was unable to turn its wealth to account. Why was this the case? The country needed peace, enterprise and capital, which it never secured until it fell under British administration.

78. **Government Service.** In dealing with the occupations and careers open to the people of India, one cannot wholly exclude the appointments which the service of the State affords. But they are altogether insignificant by the side of the great professions and industries, which not only employ far larger numbers of men, but also pay them salaries and profits much in excess of public salaries. The requirements of government do not expand as fast as those of business and commerce. It is true that, as population increases and trade extends, more courts and more public offices are needed. But, on the other hand, the State is constantly divesting itself of patronage in favour of municipal and other boards entrusted with administrative powers. It often happens that some of the highest appointments which government can bestow, as for instance the Judgeships of the High Court, are declined by successful barristers, who find at the bar a practice more lucrative than the pay of a Puisne judge. A popular physician would not be content with the salary of a district surgeon. The larger banks, the mills, and the stock exchange offer higher rewards to success than the State can pay. At the

same time while official salaries have lost their command of the market, other changes have occurred to diminish the attractions of the public service. In Persia, China, and other countries which surround India, public appointments are mainly sought for the opportunities they afford of making a fortune, and for the dignity and display attached to them. But in India the public servant receives his fixed salary without perquisites or other advantages.

Nevertheless, the service of government is honourable, and although many successful men prefer business or a profession to it, there is a keen competition for every public appointment. The struggle is so intense that it is well to bear in mind that the State after all employs an insignificant proportion of the population of India. When the last returns were prepared, showing the number of persons employed by the British government in British India in civil appointments, the total number returned was 132,852 persons. Out of this number 7991 were Europeans, and 5347 were Eurasians, the latter being principally employed in the railway and telegraph departments. It is obvious that a single industry like cotton can do more to find work and profit for the population of India than government can do with the whole of its public patronage. When one recollects that the annual trade of India by land and sea is valued at 214 crores of rupees, one can realize what an army of tradesmen, business men, and workmen is engaged in it.

79. **Emigration and Factory Laws.** It has been shown that the industrial prosperity of the country depends largely upon the freedom of labour and the ability of the working population to enter upon new

fields of industry and labour whenever their interests require a change of occupation. The less that the State interferes the better. Whatever one class of workmen have lost by the loss of one trade has been made up to them by the opening of another and more profitable business. To the mass of the people who require to buy any article, its supply at a cheaper rate is a clear gain, while to the few who lose their hereditary occupation other means of subsistence are opened. So long as the peace of India is maintained and foreign capital is attracted, fresh occupations are constantly being provided. Government must for the most part confine its attention to the main objects of keeping the public peace, improving the means of communication, and giving all the information required to promote enterprise and attract capital. But with these means supplied it can wisely leave labour to itself. To this general rule there is one exception. When foreign countries desire to enlist Indian labour, as in the case of Demerara, Trinidad, Jamaica, Mauritius, Natal, Fiji, or Surinam, the British government watches the interests of emigrants, and enforces rules for their comfort during the voyage and for their safe return with their earnings. In the same way, it interferes on behalf of labourers migrating to Assam or elsewhere if the need arises. Its sole object is to prevent any ill-treatment of the labourers or any misunderstanding as to the terms of their engagements. This principle is occasionally extended, as in the case of factory laws, so as to protect the weak and young from excessive labour, or to guard against accidents arising from defective machinery. But the secret of the success which the British government has achieved in multiplying the occupations and industries of the empire lies in giving labour free play. From the year 1843, when slavery was abolished in India, the authorities have never faltered in their policy of maintaining peace and the freedom of labour, and attracting foreign capital so as to give the population other means of livelihood than those which the cultivation of the soil can afford.

CHAPTER IX.

THE PUBLIC PEACE.

80. **Forces of Order.** The first duty which devolves upon every government is that of maintaining the public peace. This entails a two-fold task, for the proper performance of which different agencies are employed. A country's external frontiers must be protected from invasion, and its internal tranquillity must also be preserved. For attaining the first of these objects governments rely upon their naval and military forces, and for the latter purpose they employ civil forces called the police. The efficiency of these combined forces is a matter of the highest importance to the people. If disorder reigns in the land, communications by post, railway, and telegraph are interrupted; the efforts of the State to promote education and the public health are paralyzed, and all the higher interests which advance moral and material progress are neglected. The evil goes deeper still. Capital, which is the life of labour, ceases to accumulate or to flow into a disturbed country, and even the simplest occupations and trades are interrupted. Distress and misery become widespread. Any one who travels

across the frontiers of India can still see a sight which was constantly witnessed in the heart of India itself before the British peace was established, namely, frontier tribes cultivating their fields with their arms by their side and their ponies ready saddled in order to provide for their masters a means of escape. In such a state of society distress is caused not only by natural causes, such as drought or flood, which man cannot prevent, but also by the waste of good crops which nature has brought to maturity. From such a calamity good governments can protect the people if they keep in efficient order the forces at their disposal. The forces of order in every civilized country are four in number, the navy, the army, the police, and the loyal citizens.

81. **Past and Present.** In an interesting lecture[1] delivered by Mr. Robert Sewell, that eminent writer on Indian dynasties and archaeology, has traced through epic poems and vedic hymns, through inscriptions on Asoka's pillars, upon the sculptures of caves and rock-cut temples, and through scattered relics of Indian history and song, the ever recurring tale of civil strife and internal warfare which every century of Indian life discloses. His researches show that India in the dim past was a prey to the same sufferings which later historians have described. From sea to sea, and from the Himalayas to Cape Comorin, the empire was divided into a number of kingdoms which rose and fell, and for only a brief space of time maintained their power by force of arms. These kingdoms were constantly at war with each other. The country's own forces never combined to resist a foreign foe. India's richest cities were

[1] See "India before the British" in *Asiatic Quarterly Review* for July, 1897, page 120.

sacked, and her plains flowed with the blood of her children, because their weapons were turned against each other. When a foreign foe attacked the country it had no union or strength to resist. All this has been changed in the nineteenth century. Indian and British troops now stand shoulder to shoulder on the distant confines of the empire, ready to face a foreign foe and protect their homes from invasion. The wars of India which the future historian will recount are not the civil wars of the Râmâyana or the Mahâ Bhârata. They are waged against the martial races which surround Hindustan, and the military strength of the country is no longer employed against the native chiefs or the populations of India. An unarmed civil force keeps order in the interior, and the implements of war are reserved for the country's enemies who seek to disturb its peace. The two marked features which distinguish the present from the past, are the establishment of a civil police, and the application of the naval and military resources of the empire to their proper object of averting invasion or repelling a foreign foe.

82. **Naval Power.** Look at a map of India, and you will see how large a part of it is washed by the sea. Where are the capital cities of the empire, with their wealth of building and factories now situated? They face either the sea, or a river which can be navigated by ships that traverse the ocean. But you must take even a wider survey, and observe how the Indian ocean communicates with the Atlantic, and finds a passage through the Red Sea into the Mediterranean. It was on the distant Mediterranean coast that one of the decisive battles of India was fought, and won by the victory achieved by Nelson over the French

Admiral Bruey, on the 1st of August, 1798. The fall of Seringapatam, on the 4th of May, 1799, and the restoration of the Hindu dynasty of the Wadeyars to the throne of Mysore, were not entirely brought about by the victories gained on land by the British and their native allies. The naval victory of the battle of the Nile, when 11 French vessels of the line were captured, and 3,500 Frenchmen killed or wounded, was the blow which shattered the hopes of Tippu, and of the French nation. The dangers of the past may become the dangers of the future; and India, if she desires to remain a free country, must henceforth fix her eyes upon the seas, as well as upon the countries which lie over her land-frontiers. The Mahomedan emperors in vain sought to defend the coasts of India by engaging the services of the Hubshis from the African coast. The servant became the master, and turned pirate on his own account. India has now learnt to rely upon herself for her naval defence, and with the aid of the British navy scattered over the world, she is in a position to guard her shores against any attacks of hostile fleets. This boast could never have been uttered at any previous period of Indian history. Sailors are needed as well as ships, and sailors learn their trade in merchant ships as well as in vessels of war. We must not therefore exclude from any review of India's naval power, the important fact that a single company, the great Peninsular and Oriental Steam Navigation Company, employs 1,800 Lascars as deck hands, and 2,900 engine-room hands, in addition to some 2,300 men in its service who are on leave. The British India Steam Navigation Company, the Anchor Line,

H.M.S. RAMILLIES.

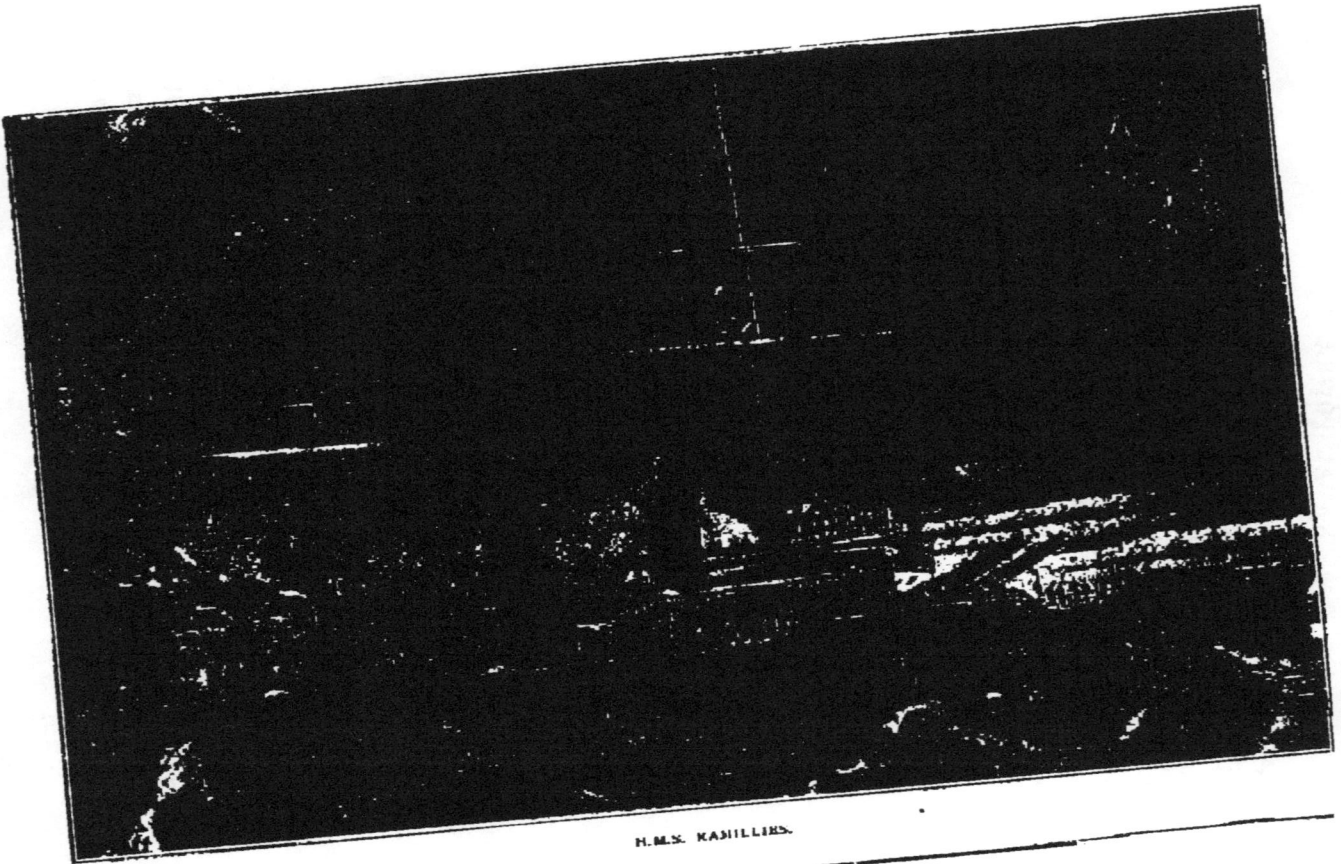

and other similar companies are also training Indian sailors. This force, which has proved its high value in storm and shipwreck, constitutes an important reserve of sea-power, taken from India itself, and trained by the British.

83. **The Naval Defence of India.** The naval forces of India consist of three lines of defence. For all parts of the British empire and its possessions, the navy of Great Britain performs its duties of watch and ward in distant seas. Ships of the largest size, such as those which are employed in western waters are never seen on the coasts of India, but the reader may form some idea of their cost and magnitude when he learns that the "Ramillies," which is the flag-ship employed in the Mediterranean Sea, cost £875,000 (nearly one and a half crores of rupees), and there are many other battleships of the first class which are similar to it. It has a speed of 17·5 knots an hour, and carries 1800 tons of coal, with a complement of officers and men numbering 730. The thickness of its armour on the side is 18·5 inches, and it is armed with 61 guns, of which ten are quick-firing 10·6 inch guns, and seven torpedo tubes. Its indicated horse-power is 13,000, and the vessel is 380 feet long, and 75 feet on the beam. It is not easy to realize from this description the power of this battleship, but if you compare the particulars given with those of the largest vessel you have ever seen, you can form some idea of it.

The second and nearer line of naval defence is supplied by the imperial cruisers, gun-boats, torpedo boats, and turret-ships, employed by Great Britain on the East Indies Station. Other nations, France, Italy, Turkey and Portugal have their own ships in Eastern waters; and in the Persian Gulf, to which Indian trade and commerce are carried, there are many petty chiefs who, were it not for the protection afforded to Indian ships by British vessels, would inflict serious injury upon Indian subjects. In fact piracy prevailed in these quarters until in quite recent years it was suppressed by the British.

Lastly, there are the vessels belonging to the Indian government, largely manned by natives of India, which patrol the tidal rivers, carry troops, make surveys and watch the ports of India. It has been necessary to dwell on these facts, because few citizens of India adequately realize the large part which vessels of war play in the defence of their country, and in the extension of their commerce.

84. **The Military Forces.** The army consists of some 206,000 men, exclusive of the Hyderabad contingent and of the forces of the native states. Of this Imperial army some 73,000 are Europeans, whose ranks are regularly kept up to their proper strength by constant recruitment from England. Should the need arise, additional drafts can be drawn from Great Britain; but the expense of an efficient army is so great that the government wisely employs no more than it requires at the time for the defence of the empire. The figures given above convey an imperfect idea of the defensive resources of India. Without ready means of transport an army must waste its time and strength in inaction. Without equipments constantly renewed, and without arms of the best and most improved fashion, the bravest soldiers cannot turn their fighting qualities to the best account. Fortifications and coast defences, bridges and railways,

arsenals and powder factories, cost more than the pay of a whole army-corps, but they add an incalculable value to the defence afforded to India by its soldiers. It is in the combination of living power with control over, and with a proper use of, physical difficulties, that India possesses to-day a military strength which vastly exceeds anything that it ever possessed before. Science has enabled the British Government to rely upon an army which in point of numbers is inferior to the undisciplined hordes which overran the country in olden times. But discipline, skill, and organisation have so raised the standard and efficiency of the fighting force, that a small army led by British officers, and supplied with the latest improvements of military science, is able to defend the long frontier of India, and to support, when the need arises, the civil police.

Behind the imperial forces stand the armies of the native states, bound alike by their own interests and by their treaties to regard the foes of the British Government as their own foes, and to employ all their resources against them. But the old idea, that large armies without discipline and training can prevail against a small well-organized force, has been proved to be an error upon many a battlefield in India. Accordingly, some of the leading states have undertaken to supply one or more regiments for the defence of the empire, and they seek the advice and help of a British officer in keeping them in a state ready for instant service. These are called imperial-service troops, and they belong to the following states, Kashmir, Patiala, Bahawalpur, Jind, Nabha, Kapurthala, Faridkote, Alwar, Bhartpur, Jodhpur, Gwalior, Bhopal, Indore, Rampur, Hyderabad, Mysore,

Sirmur, Maler Kotla, Bikanir, and three states (Bhavnagar, Junagad, and Navanagar) in Kathiawar. To make these forces quite efficient they require not only transport, but also that supply of medical officers and equipment which is essential in time of war.

Volunteers must also be mentioned in any account of the military strength of India. But the conditions of England, where the volunteer force has attained its largest proportion, and those of India are widely diverse. A volunteer force being drawn from the ranks of men, who are engaged in their civil occupations and trades, cannot well serve at any great distance from the scene of their ordinary vocations. The distances in an empire so large as India are enormous, and the system of caste and the numerous divisions of Indian society involve difficulties in combined action which would greatly reduce the usefulness of volunteers. In the small hill district of Coorg, which lies far removed from the garrisons in the plains, a useful field exists for the employment of volunteers, and in many of the cities of India there are opportunities for turning the movement to good account. There are about 29,000 volunteers enrolled in India, but their efficiency varies greatly in different parts of the country.

85. **Civil Police.** For maintaining the internal peace of India, the military forces just described can be relied upon if need arises, but the task of preserving the public tranquillity rests primarily upon the law, the magistrates, and the civil police. In the times of the Mahomedan emperors the civil and the military command rested in the same hands. The governors of the provinces were also the commanders-in-chief,

and soldiers regularly performed duties which are now entrusted to police officers and constables. In the early days of British rule the native system was not at once changed, and even now, when a new province or district is annexed to the empire, order is at first maintained by soldiers. Then after an interval, the dacoits and bands of organized robbers, who usually profit by the disorder caused by recent war, are dealt with by a force which is half military and half civil. Such are the military police still employed in parts of Upper Burma. Finally a purely civil force takes their place. The civil police are for the most part not armed with anything more formidable than a truncheon. They are subject to the ordinary law, and if they use unlawful violence they are themselves sent to prison. They are chosen from the ranks of the people amongst whom they serve. They are only drilled occasionally, and they act singly or in small parties, and not in large bodies like soldiers.

86. **The Policeman's Finger.** In London, even at times when the streets are thronged by millions of foot passengers, or blocked by lines of carriages all anxious to get forward, an unarmed constable can at once stop traffic, or direct its course, by the mere raising of his finger. He is able to do so because the people have a respect for law, and know that the orders of a solitary policeman are issued in the name and in the strength of the law. No doubt troublesome persons, and especially those guilty of breaking the law, resent his interference, and at times they resist him. But there are always many citizens ready to interfere and support his authority. Sensible people know that it is to their own interest to place themselves on the side of

public order, and to assist the police in maintaining it. The man who refuses to obey the civil police when they are discharging their duty refuses to obey the law, and public opinion in well-ordered countries rallies on the side of order. If once it is admitted that the public peace must at all hazards be preserved, then there are only two courses open to the authorities. The military may be employed to break down disorder by force and bloodshed, or the gentler pressure of a civil police may be used to prevent matters going so far as to create disorder. The people in British India who have passed all their lives under the blessing of peace can hardly realize what civil wars and martial order mean. At rare intervals, when classes are unusually excited against each other, troops are called in for a few hours to assist the police. But if the peace should not be instantly restored by such means, it would become necessary to adopt sterner methods; and it is unwise to risk the perils of martial law. The policeman's finger carries with it a double warning. It is raised in the name of the civil law, and disobedience means a breach of that law. But it also warns those who would disregard it that behind the police stand other forces of order, the trained troops who can never be called into action without arms in their hands and cartridges in their pouches.

87. **Punitive Police.** There is one great difference between the soldiers and the police. The former are what is called an imperial force, and the latter are a provincial or local force. In other words, the whole of the military forces are under one central authority, the government of India, which can direct their movements from one centre, and unite or divide the fighting power

of India as it pleases. The police belong to and are employed by the provincial governments, or sometimes by cantonment committees. There is no fixed proportion of police either to the population or area. The police force in Bombay, 23,507 men, is rather larger than that employed in Madras, 22,088 men. In the North-Western Provinces it is larger (25,700 men) than in Bengal, where 23,600 men suffice. Where there are several native states into which criminals may escape out of British jurisdiction, or where the disorderly members of society are more numerous, a large force is required. The cost must be provided by the province, or by the cantonment, which employs the men. Sometimes, however, in a particular village, city, or area, the local residents commit a series of offences against the public peace with which the ordinary police force cannot contend. Then, it is not fair that the general taxpayer, or the inhabitants of other towns and places which are orderly, should be taxed to provide additional police in order to keep the peace in a locality where it is broken by the bad conduct of a few. Accordingly, additional police are engaged by government to serve in the disturbed tract, and those who have either caused or weakly connived at the disturbances are properly made to pay for their employment. They are called punitive police because they are paid for by the persons assessed as a punishment.

88. **The People.** The strongest of all the forces of order which a country can employ for its own internal defence are the good sense and co-operation of its own people. It is not easy to exaggerate the influence for peace and order which the citizens can themselves

exert. In England respect for authority and regard for the religious beliefs and feelings of others are part of the national character. They are the best allies to the police. If large crowds are disposed to obey the law and the commands of the constables, the chances of collision are reduced to a minimum. If the public press in times of excitement refrains from publishing false rumours or attacks upon lawful authority, the people will readily take their tone from it. There is yet another way in which citizens can help to improve the efficiency of the police. They can refuse to tempt them by bribes, and can report at once to their superior officers any neglect of their duties. By loyally obeying the lawful commands of the police, and by bringing to notice any irregularities of which they are guilty, the public not only render recourse to military aid unnecessary, but they constantly improve the character and discipline of the constabulary. The behaviour of the police depends to a large extent upon the behaviour of the people amongst whom they work. Those who condemn the native police of India should ask themselves how far they and their fellow-citizens are to blame for any defects and abuses that may be found in the ranks of a force, which is drawn from native society, and must be influenced to a large extent by the state of local feeling.

CHAPTER X.

THE PUBLIC HEALTH.

89. **Science.** A wise and good government calls in the aid of science not only to destroy but to save life. In the last chapter we have seen that the strength of the army in India rests less upon numbers than upon a judicious application to the art of war of the teachings of science. In the constant training of the British officers, in the supply of the most precise arms and the latest and best equipments, and in its treatment of natural and physical difficulties, lies the superiority of the military force of India. Consider, for instance, how the obstacles of nature are sometimes turned to advantage, and at other times overcome. Rivers and mountains are sometimes of great value in selecting sites for forts, and in defending frontiers against an enemy. At other times a mountain which arrests the movement of an army is pierced by a tunnel, and the Indus itself is crossed by a bridge at Sukkur, which is a triumph of engineering science. The electric current, which kills on the spot the person who incautiously touches it, is harmlessly employed to carry man's messages over land and

sea from one end of the world to the other. Powder, which kills those who handle it without care, is made by scientific use to level the walls of a city or to spread death amongst the enemy. In these and other ways science helps man to defend himself or to kill his foes. But happily science is not less powerful as a means of saving life and improving the health and happiness of mankind.

90. **Ignorance.** Its usefulness in this direction is sometimes impaired by false notions and widespread ignorance. It is therefore the duty of government to educate the people, and to teach them by experience how injuries can be repaired, illnesses cured, and the spread of disease checked by their own efforts. If any one should walk carelessly into an open well and so break his leg or kill himself, we should be justified in blaming him for his misfortune. The issues of life and death are in the hands of Providence, but God has given to men understanding and eyes and limbs in order to enable them to take care of their lives and bodies. A religious person should hesitate to blame Providence for misfortunes which proper attention and precaution could have prevented. Science has shown plainly that polluted water, unclean linen, and a disregard of sanitary laws, produce germs of death and disease. The Aryans of old laid great stress on purifications, and the Mahomedans hold the tenet that "Cleanliness is the key of heaven." But people are prone to forget, and to overlook, what is not apparent to the naked eye. Without a microscope or the scientific apparatus which enables a medical man to see with his eye in a drop of dirty water the microbes or living organisms which spread cholera, pestilence, and

other mortal ailments, we are apt to deny their existence. But the microbes are there none the less, and whether we see them or not they kill us mercilessly. We ought, therefore, to avoid polluted water. Clean linen in dressing wounds is as important as clean water. Some few years ago certain hospitals in Europe were condemned to be pulled down and rebuilt because it was believed that their very boards and walls were hopelessly impregnated with germs of disease. But Lord Lister discovered that a slight change in the dressing of wounds, and absolute cleanliness in the lint applied and in the instruments used, were sufficient to arrest the mortality; and the very hospitals which had been condemned are now amongst the most healthy institutions in the land. In these and other instances the discoveries made by medical science under the blessing of Providence have proved to be as beneficial to man as the discovery of steam or the telegraph or electricity. India can now enjoy with Europe the advantages of these modern inventions, and the governments of the various provinces have undertaken, as far as their means will allow, to bring them within easy reach of the people of India. It is therefore our own fault if through ignorance or prejudice we deprive ourselves of the benefits which science has bestowed on us.

91. **Hospitals**. One of the first steps taken by the British authorities in India was to build hospitals and dispensaries where injured and sick persons could be treated. Many of the rulers of the native states have not been slow to follow their example. The popularity of these institutions increases from year to year, but there are still many ignorant

persons in India who forget that none but the very sick go into hospital, and attribute the deaths which must occur in them, not to the hopeless condition of the patients, but to the fault of the medical officers. This prejudice is not shared to the same degree by the wild tribes which live beyond the frontiers of India. Whenever a mission is sent to explore their country,

THE WALTER HOSPITAL, BUILT BY H.H. THE MAHARAJAH OF UDAIPUR, RAJPUTANA.

or to mark out boundaries outside British India, the medical officer attached to it finds himself surrounded at all hours by numerous patients clamouring for his help, whether in the performance of operations or in the prescription of medicine. In the same way dispensaries and hospitals on the confines of the British empire are largely attended by Pathans, Baluchis, Chinese, and others, who thoroughly appreciate their benefits. In India itself the mistrust of hospitals varies according to the education and prejudices of the people. Thus it is less marked in Bombay than in Bengal. But since any one is at liberty to visit a hospital, and the friends of patients can see for themselves how the sick are treated, a more trustful spirit must slowly extend itself, and it is satisfactory to know that already 2211 institutions are working in India, which annually receive 348,000 in-patients, and give relief to 18,588,000 out-patients. The attendance in Bengal is far below that in the North-Western Provinces, or in the Punjab or Madras, and slightly below that in Bombay. When the smaller population of Bombay is taken into account, it will be found that in no other part of India are the hospitals more largely attended.

92. **Lady Dufferin.** No one even in Europe enters a hospital with feelings of pleasure. People submit to the necessity only because they are persuaded in their own minds that certain injuries and maladies can be treated there with greater skill and more attention to nursing than the patients can command in their own houses. One cannot expect that a natural repugnance to hospitals should be easily overcome by an effort of reason in the case of women and children. The customs of the East are also opposed to the use of public institutions by women who are expected to live in seclusion. It is inevitable that the young should look upon a hospital with feelings of terror, and indulgent parents are apt to yield too much to the natural wishes of their children. Can then nothing be done for the female and younger members of society when they are suffering pain which medical science could alleviate?

This question presented itself to the wife of the Indian viceroy when the Marquis of Dufferin and

MARCHIONESS OF DUFFERIN AND AVA.

Ava filled that exalted post. The name of Lady Dufferin will for ever be associated with a scheme of

relief which will provide a widespread remedy when its value is more fully appreciated. Lady Dufferin devised a plan for founding in some places hospitals for women and children, and for supplying there and elsewhere trained native nurses who might take their services to the houses where they were required. A large measure of success has already attended both parts of her scheme. As an instance of the former may be mentioned the hospital at Amraoti, which in its first year gave relief to 6215 out-patients and 96 in-door patients. In several parts of India nurses are being trained, and there exists a large demand for their services. It is hoped that one day every large town or village in India will send to the hospitals a few native women to learn the art of nursing, and thence to return to their homes and give their help to their neighbours in time of need. In order that the plan may be successful, endeavours are made to form local committees to collect and allot funds for the purposes mentioned. Several native chiefs and wealthy citizens have taken a warm interest in Lady Dufferin's proposals, and there can be no doubt that when the nursing scheme has been given a fair trial it will spread rapidly, and so place within reach of medical relief a number of sufferers who have the strongest claims upon the sympathy of men.

93. **Prevention of Disease.** It is well said that prevention is better than cure, and the Indian governments do not content themselves with providing hospitals, dispensaries, or nurses. Science has shown how certain diseases which used to ravage India can be prevented or curtailed. Of these diseases, which used to sweep away their hundreds of thousands every

year, small-pox was once the most dreaded. But human nature is the same in the West and in the East, and just as vaccination has practically expelled small-pox from Europe, so the same results may be expected from the adoption of the same methods in India. Some 30 per cent. of the children born every year in India are now vaccinated, and as the people learn by experience the wonderful success of this simple remedy, one may expect that in a few years a much larger percentage of children will be protected from the risk of catching small-pox.

Amongst other measures taken by the British government to prevent disease the most important are the provision of a pure water-supply, the improvement of systems of drainage and conservancy, and the constitution of sanitary boards. Many crores of rupees have been spent in the cities and large towns of India on bringing from a distant and unpolluted source, through clean channels or pipes, a liberal supply of drinking water for the people. Some opposition was at first shown to this excellent reform. But in every case where the stagnant wells and tanks, into which the rain water or the drains used to flow, have ceased to be used by the people, the death-rate has instantly fallen in the most remarkable manner. Much has still to be done in the villages, but every effort should be made by the people themselves to induce the villagers to keep the wells from which they draw their drinking water separate from those used for bathing or washing purposes. In the same way, both in municipalities and villages, increased attention is being paid to the removal of sewerage and rubbish. In order to advise public bodies or individuals, a sanitary board of expert officers has been organized in most provinces, and under the influence of these several measures deaths from cholera, dysentery, and fever, which collectively still number about six millions a year, have in ordinary seasons been sensibly reduced.

94. **Famine Relief.** In exceptional years of scarcity caused by failure of rains, the British government organizes a campaign against famine on a most extended scale. The whole forces of the empire are then called out and employed to fight an enemy, against which no previous government in India ever attempted to lift a finger. In former days the authorities considered themselves powerless, and those of the suffering masses who escaped death emerged from a famine as the bond-slaves of men to whom they had sold themselves or their families in return for food. Now, however, government undertakes to relieve the destitute, and to restore those who survive the hardships of famine to their freedom and their ordinary occupations. The measures taken to secure this object follow the lines upon which disease is attacked, namely prevention and cure. The absolute prevention of all famines is beyond the power of man. Men cannot forbid the clouds of locusts to gather, or even altogether restrain floods, or prevent a plague of rats. Still less can they bid the rains to fall if Providence withholds the usual monsoon. Famines must therefore recur in parts of India unless the climate is altered. But a great deal can be done to prevent scarcity becoming a famine, or a real famine assuming the proportions which, as we learn from history, they reached in the eighteenth and earlier centuries.

Some of these preventive measures may be explained. Science helps here, as she does in vaccination and in the art of military defence. Information is collected throughout the year by a meteorological department as to the snow-fall, the course of storms, currents, and winds, and the conditions of atmosphere prevailing in the seas and countries beyond India. The surface of the sun, and its spots, are also examined, and by all these means some forecast is possible of the probable character of the next monsoon. According to the estimate, arrangements are then made to carry out a programme of work in case the rain should fail. Above all, with a prospect of famine before them, people begin to economise their consumption of grain. A more certain measure of prevention is the extension, as far as possible, of works of irrigation; but even if the water required could be collected, it is not always possible to use it without exhausting the soil or making the ground waterlogged and malarious. Still an immense deal has been done in recent years, and out of 197 millions of cultivated acres, exclusive of certain tracts in British India for which no returns are given, more than ten millions are irrigated by canals for which full accounts are kept, while by means of tanks a similar area is supplied with water. It is computed that food supplies for 120 millions of people are ensured by these measures of protection. Railways are the next great means of prevention, and the British government has opened 20,110 miles of railroad in India, thus enabling food to be carried to the starving people, and allowing part of the population to leave the afflicted tracts. Nor must we overlook the care bestowed upon the forests of India, which cover 131,000 square miles, and whose conservancy exercises a powerful effect upon the rainfall. If the hillsides are stript of their trees, nature's chief influence in creating and retaining moisture and in attracting clouds is impaired. By these means several seasons of scarcity, which would formerly have become years of famine, have in recent years been tided over.

95. **Freedom of Trade.** In former times, when famine threatened a certain state or province, the cry was raised that the export of grain must be prohibited, and that the government must itself buy and import grain. Experience has, however, proved the mischief of this course, except in very rare circumstances where communications are defective and trading enterprise unusually weak. Where scarcity is widespread, the co-operation of hundreds and thousands of traders is needed. If government does not interfere with them, their own self-interest will induce them to buy and sell as much grain as they can collect from outside, and dispose of it to the people. But if government competes, private traders become alarmed and stand aloof. Their co-operation is lost, and public officers, having other duties to perform, are sure to find the task of general supply beyond their powers. No doubt government can bring a large supply into a particular city, but the news of its arrival at once attracts a huge mob of starving people, and in their vain efforts to get what they want, thousands are crushed or excluded. The distribution of food in a great number of centres is essential to a proper system of relief, and that can only be secured by encouraging many independent agencies to work heartily in their own interests without the competition or interference

of government. But the State can, and should, assist their efforts by collecting and publishing accurate figures, in order to show the number of people to be fed, the prices that are being paid in various centres, and the out-turn of crops in parts which are not affected by famine. With railways and good roads, and with the growth of capital and competition amongst traders, private trade, when duly informed on these points, can effect much more than the State. Freedom of trade is thus a powerful agency both in the prevention and in the cure of famines.

96. **Work and Charity**. On the 16th of June, 1897, the official accounts showed that 4,240,337 persons were on relief in India. Some were described as on "test work," a larger number on "relief works," and others "on gratuitous relief." Work with pay for all who can possibly handle a spade or carry a basket, and charity for the infirm, the sick, or those who cannot do manual labour: these are the sound principles of famine relief. It is sometimes argued that it is harsh to enforce work from those who are not accustomed to work. But a little consideration shows that work is as advantageous to the people as to the State. It is as good for the bodies as for the minds of those who need relief. The body, though weak, is kept in health by moderate exercise, and the self-respect of famine stricken people is preserved by feeling that they are giving something in return for the wages they receive. The labourers are thus not pauperized by receiving charity. There is yet another reason for dividing the famine stricken people into labour gangs. They are by this means placed in their proper places without confusion. They fall into the

ranks of a well-drilled army of workmen, and their health and the payment of their wages can be properly looked after. This is no small matter when many thousands of people are collected together in a single place.

But the arrangement is beneficial also to the nation and the community at large. The cost of famine relief is an enormous charge upon public revenues, that is to say, upon the taxpayers of India, and at a time when land-revenue is being remitted or its collection deferred, the last state would be worse than the first if the country should ruin itself, or saddle itself with an unnecessary load of debt in order to fight one year of famine. Accordingly the "test works" described above, at which wages or relief are in the first stages of famine offered only to men willing to work, afford a valuable indication of the need for relief. So long as the wages paid are just sufficient to keep the workmen in health, public charity will not be abused by men who can support themselves. The works attract those, and those only, who are in absolute need. Economy is secured not merely by keeping the wages down and imposing labour as a condition of relief: something is also saved to the State in the shape of the work done. When the "test work" proves that relief on a large scale is really needed, then the workmen are sent to "relief works." Perhaps a railway embankment is made, a canal excavated, or a reservoir constructed. The labourers are, it is true, weak, and their work is not worth the full amount of the wages which must be paid to them; but it is worth something, and thus the taxpayer, who has to pay the bill for famine relief, gets some compensation for the heavy charges which he has to meet. That gratuitous relief and charity should be given to those who from age or infirmity or other good causes cannot work is fully recognized; but the principle that a fair day's labour should be given by those who require relief and can work, is merely an act of justice to the taxpayer and a benefit to the people relieved.

97. **Plague.** At rare intervals a sudden and terrible illness may break out, which, like the "black death" or the "bubonic plague," may threaten to destroy whole cities and bring ruin upon the survivors. On such occasions it is the duty of government to save the people even against their own wills, if the magnitude of the danger is sufficiently great. In 1896 a few cases of plague appeared in the city of Bombay, and before many months had passed half the population had fled in terror, carrying with them to other parts of India the terrible disease which pursued them in their flight. The plague, which might have been confined to a single city, by these means established itself in several centres. No locality suffered more than Kutch, where prompt measures were not taken to separate those who were attacked, or their friends amongst whom they died, from the healthy population. The relatives of the deceased carried the infection to others, and the mortality was terrible. Far wiser was the treatment of a village in the territory of Gwalior, around which the troops of His Highness the Maharaja Sindhia were at once drawn, and no one was allowed to move from the infected area until the risk of contagion had passed. The effects of leaving a disease like the bubonic plague to go its own way deserve the careful thought of all men. In the first place, infection spreads and destroys human life, as a jungle fire

devours all that is before it when steps are not taken to isolate it. In the next place, the most distant nations, severed from India by continents or seas, take alarm, and refuse to buy the products or manufactures of a country infected with the dreaded disease. The industry and occupations of hundreds of thousands of healthy people are thus paralyzed, and it takes many years before trade returns to its old course or confidence is re-established. It becomes then the duty of government to intervene where such vital interests are at stake. Whether persons attacked by the plague like it or not, they must be compelled to go to hospital, and their friends and relations who have been living with them must be separated from the rest of the population. The duty which devolves upon government is very painful, but it is quite clear, and the whole empire looks to it to perform its task with resolution and promptitude. There is no civilized country in the world in which the obligation of the State to employ its powers to prevent the spread of plague is not fully recognized. By no other means can lives be saved, and the ruin of industries and trade be averted.

98. **Public Markets.** An outbreak of plague can only be dealt with by government with all the resources at its back. But there are other bodies, especially municipalities, which can render constant service to health by a judicious use of their powers of self-government. Pure water does much for health, but the purity of food should also not be neglected. To mix impure water with milk, or to expose articles of food in dirty stalls and unwashed markets, are frequently the means of spreading cholera and other diseases. For this reason most municipalities build public market-places,

where traders can sell their goods under proper conditions of cleanliness and free air. It is a convenience to the public to have one place set apart for the purchase of their vegetables and other supplies; but apart from this, a public market can, under proper regulations, be kept tidy and clean, and the opportunity is afforded of inspecting supplies and seeing that unwholesome articles are not exposed for sale. In these and many other directions the British government, while leaving the people free to buy or sell what they please, endeavours to prevent the spread of diseases and to improve the public health. But after all, government can never do as much for the health of the people as they can do for themselves, and it is therefore the duty of every citizen to learn the value of cleanliness, and to practise it not only in his own interests, but in the interests of the families which surround him.

CHAPTER XI.

PUBLIC INCOME AND EXPENDITURE.

99. **The Public Purse.** The management of a bank or of any large business requires both ability and experience, and it would be no easy task to explain its system to a school-boy. But the difficulty is much increased when one attempts to set before the reader some idea of the financial arrangements of a vast empire, which has an annual income from public revenues of 95 crores. It is, however, very necessary that the citizen of India, who pays taxes and rates, should know what becomes of them. The government of India is constantly publishing for his information in the official gazettes statements of revenue and expenditure, and some attempt ought to be made at school to teach the young what they mean.

Let us first consider the position of government. It holds the public purse for the country, and receives and spends all income derived from the public property in land or railways, as well as the taxes paid by the people. By means of these supplies it carries on the administration, and if the people, or any section of them, ask for more schools, more courts, or more public works, then the funds required for the purpose must be provided either by additional taxation, or else by reducing expenditure elsewhere. It must be remembered that the government of India puts into the public purse something more than mere taxes. It is able to do so because it acts in numerous capacities. It owns the land and receives rents or assessments. Some of these rents, called assignments, it collects and passes on to the persons entitled to them. It takes charge of deposits and performs the part of banker for others. It issues notes, and contracts loans which it generally lays out as capital expenditure in the construction of railways or irrigation works. It produces and sells salt and opium, it carries the post and sends messages by telegraph, and it constructs and works railways and canals, from all of which sources the public purse is supplied. It is thus evident that its operations are complicated and extensive, and in order that the taxpayer may know exactly what becomes of the money which is received on his behalf by the State, the information is given to him in the shape of a budget. We must then consider what is meant by a budget.

100. **Budget Estimates and Accounts.** The government of India reckons its financial year from the 1st of April to the 31st of March following. Before the year begins, it calculates what it expects to receive and what it expects to spend. The calculation is shown in a balance sheet called the *budget estimate.* As the months of the year roll by, it becomes evident that the receipts expected

from this or that head of revenue will be more or less than the estimate. Perhaps a famine occurs and rents are not paid, or the rate of exchange falls, or a war adds to expenses, or the traffic on the railways falls off. The financial department, which feels the pulse of the public accounts and receives reports from all the treasuries in the empire, revises the budget estimates accordingly; and before the year is closed *revised estimates* are published. Finally, when the year has passed, and the complete accounts of the various provinces and districts are received, *the accounts* of the past year are published. By these means the public are continually being informed what income and expenditure the government anticipates, then the information is corrected by the light of experience, and finally it is announced what was received and spent in the year. The description which has been given in this book of the village, the district, the province, and the empire, will enable any one to follow the process by which this result is obtained. A raiyat, for instance, is assessed on his holding at 5 rupees, payable in a certain village. The village accountant sends this estimate to the subdivision, whence it goes to the district, and so to the provincial capital, from which it is forwarded to the financial department of the supreme government. Five rupees on the account stated is accordingly entered under the head of "land revenue" in the budget. But the monsoon fails and the first instalment of the assessment is not paid. Accordingly the original estimate is reduced to three rupees, and in the revised estimates there is a deduction of two rupees. But, again, the later harvest is favourable, and the raiyat finally pays his full assessment, and the accounts show it accordingly. It is only necessary to add that in the budget and the accounts, the symbol or notation of **Rx** is used. This means tens of rupees, and if ten silver rupees were equal to one English gold pound, as they once were, a crore of rupees would equal one million pounds.

101. **Taxes and Rates.** If we omit the proceeds of loans, the public revenue available for expenditure may be said to consist of payments for services rendered, and of taxes and rates. Taxes again are either direct or indirect. *Direct taxes* are taxes levied on the persons intended to pay them. The person who pays assessed taxes such as the income tax, the purchaser of stamps, he who registers a deed, and the raiyat who contributes provincial rates, pay direct taxes. *Indirect taxes* are advanced by the person who pays them in the expectation that he will recover what he has advanced from another. Ignorant people often fail to understand that they are paying an indirect tax. Instances of indirect taxes are excise, customs, and tolls. By *excise* is meant an indirect tax levied on the production of an article in India; by *customs*, a similar tax levied on importation of goods into India, and by *tolls*, one levied on the conveyance of an article. If a petty shopkeeper sells European cloth in a village in the interior of the country, he must charge his customer a price which will cover the price of the cloth at the factory in Europe, and the charges for its conveyance from Europe to his shop, together with the customs duty paid in Bombay and any tolls which

may have been paid on the roads. The purchaser thus repays the taxes to the shopkeeper.

It is the right of government to levy taxes, but, as we have seen in a previous chapter, municipal committees are authorised by it to levy local taxation for local purposes. The taxes imposed by them are called *rates*. Sometimes the State collects for local bodies a local cess based on the land assessment. Such collections are shown under provincial rates.

102. **Principles of Taxation.** The British government introduced into India the system of budgets, and some of the more advanced native states are following its example. But the reforms which it has applied to the system of taxation are of even greater value. It is now a well accepted principle that the taxes imposed by the government of India should be certa n and not arbitary, so that every one may know what he has to pay. The land settlements of every district of British India have this object in view. When former governments took from the raiyat a share of the produce, no one ever knew how much of his crop would be taken from him. Now every tenant of the State knows exactly what sum of money he has to pay.

Another principle is that the taxes should take as little as possible from the taxpayer beyond what they bring into the treasury. The numerous cesses, which used to be collected in addition to the land assessment by former rulers of India, were frequently intercepted by those who had to receive them. Such were the taxes on special articles of food, on sales or transfers, on feasts or marriages, on journeys and change of residence, and on an endless variety of objects, which have now been removed from the books of the village accountant in British India. They produced little, because the proceeds were often misappropriated. They caused annoyance and loss to the taxpayers, and restricted trade and freedom of movement. The small gain to the public purse was nothing in comparison with the loss which the people suffered. Any one who studies side by side the items of taxation in British India and those in a native state which has not altered the old system, will be struck by the long list of small taxes levied in the latter.

A third principle is that rich or influential classes should not be treated differently from the poorer citizens. As far as possible the British government endeavours to collect from the taxpayers an equal contribution in proportion to the benefits they enjoy under the protection afforded to them.

Finally, endeavours are made to return to the taxpayer in the shape of roads and public works of general usefulness a large proportion of the taxes paid.

103. **Special Advantages**. Compared with other countries the taxpayer in India is in many respects fortunate. Out of 95 crores of rupees which went into the public purse as the revenue of India for 1894-95, a year selected as being free from unusual disturbances, more than 66·5 did not come from the taxpayer in the shape of taxation. The following statement shows the sources from which this large sum was received :

Crores, 25·4 land-revenue from tenants,
„ 7·3 opium, chiefly from the Chinese consumer,
„ 1·6 forest-produce from purchasers,

Crores,	0·8	contributions from native states,
"	0·8	interest from loans,
"	2·6	postal, telegraph, and mint receipts,
"	1·6	received from civil departments,
"	1·2	miscellaneous on account of pensions, etc.,
"	21·2	railway receipts from passengers and others,
"	2·3	irrigation supplied to customers,
"	0·7	sale of stores for roads,
"	1·0	certain army receipts.
Crores,	66·5	

A few remarks will explain the position. If the holders of State-lands did not pay to government their assessments, which are after all only customary rents, they would certainly pay their rents, and probably heavier rents fixed by competition, to a private landlord. The tenants of zemindars know the truth of this statement. The cultivator of state-lands pays for the use of the land, and the taxpayer gets the benefit of his contribution to the public purse. The opium grown under favourable conditions of climate in India is chiefly bought by the Chinese, and the profits of the sales to a foreigner relieve the Indian taxpayer of so much taxation. The receipts from forests, railways, post-offices, telegraphs, and canals are all payments by persons for value received or services rendered. The civil departments collect fines, receive fees for education or medical relief, and sell stores which are not required. Thus the Indian taxpayer gains because the State owns a large landed property and other paying concerns.

104. **Special Difficulties.** On the other hand, India is liable to three peculiar difficulties, which constantly throw out its financial calculations. It cannot tell when it may please Providence to withhold the monsoons, upon which the land-revenue and the means of subsistence of those who are engaged in agriculture depend. The cost of relief when famine occurs is so heavy that it has to be met in part by raising loans. We shall presently see what other steps are annually taken to insure the country against such disasters.

A second difficulty arises from the exchange. India constructs railways, and buys the material required from the cheapest source of supply, which is Europe. It also borrows money and draws capital from Europe, both for purposes of the State, and also for its municipal, and even for private commercial, undertakings. It enlists in its service British soldiers, and it orders from abroad its war-material and stores. It pays pensions to the Europeans whose services it has employed in military or civil capacities. On all these and other accounts it has to pay bills in gold, which is the currency of the west. Since the Indian coinage is silver, and the taxes are received in rupees, gold coin has to be bought or acquired by exchange for rupees. Now the market-value of silver stated in terms of gold constantly changes, just as the market value of all other articles offered for sale is liable to change from day to day. Every one knows that the silver price of bajri or rice rises or falls according to the state of supply in the market. In the same way the gold value of a silver rupee fluctuates or changes, and although the government of India endeavours to fix a correct rate of exchange for the purpose of its budget-estimates, the market rate often falls below the rate so fixed, and there is what is called a *loss by exchange.* In the year 1894-95 the rate of exchange, as fixed in the estimates, was 14d. for a rupee, but the actual average rate realized was a little over 13d. The fall of nearly one penny added 2 crores and 12 lakhs to the charges on the public purse for the year.

Then again India is surrounded by fanatical and fighting races of men, who at times violate the frontier and break their engagements. The operations undertaken against them cost money, especially in the matter of providing transport, and unforeseen military expenditure has to be met. In former days there was a fourth danger to which India was exposed, namely a fall in the price obtained for opium. But the opium revenue has of late been so much reduced that fluctuations in it are of less consequence than they used to be.

105. **Famine Relief and Insurance.** The most serious of all the difficulties just described is that of the risk of famine. Much has been done, by extending railways, forests, and works of irrigation, to mitigate the sufferings and cost of famine. But the climate of the country cannot be altered by the wisest of governments, and therefore it is necessary to expect famines to occur from time to time and to insure against them, just as a prudent man insures against the accidents of fire or sickness. In its budget-estimates government annually provides or "appropriates" a sum for famine relief and insurance.

If famine occurs, the whole sum and much more is spent on the actual relief of famine. If it does not occur, the sum provided is invested as it accumulates, just as a bank invests its reserve fund. It is applied either to the extinction or to the avoidance of debt. Debt is extinguished by paying off a part of some loan previously contracted, or it is avoided by devoting the fund to the construction of works of a protective character. For instance, a certain line of railway may not prove a remunerative work when viewed as a means of traffic, but it may be essential to famine relief by affording the means of carrying grain in seasons of scarcity into a part of India exposed to a failure of the monsoon. The famine insurance fund would wisely be applied to the construction of such a line. It would be an excellent investment for the funds. To collect the taxes for famine insurance, and lock them up in a treasury until they were required to be doled out as famine wages or charitable grants, would be a waste of interest. By extending railways before the need for them arises, government arms itself beforehand with effective means for carrying on a famine campaign, and it attains the same object if it devotes the investment to the liquidation or avoidance of debt, because it saves the interest which it would have to pay, and thus leaves more money available to cope with famine. The famine provision figures in the budget, which is the balance sheet of the year, as an item of expenditure.

106. **The Burden of Taxation.** We have seen that if the land-revenue is treated as rent paid for the use of land, 66½ crores of the revenues of India are not strictly due to taxation. We can now

examine more closely the items which fill the public purse with the remainder of the 95 crores shown in the accounts for 1894-95.

Crores of rupees	8·7	were received	from salt,
"	4·6	"	from stamps,
"	5·5	"	from excise,
"	3·6	"	provincial rates
"	3·9	"	customs,
"	1·8	"	assessed taxes,
"	0·4	"	registration.
	28·5		

Some portion of the indirect taxes mentioned above, such as customs and salt, are paid by the subjects of natives states, but if the pressure of taxation is calculated on the basis of the population of British India as taken in 1891, with an addition of one per cent. a year as its annual increase, then every head of the population would pay an average tax to the public purse of 1R. 3as. 10p. If the land-revenue receipts are added to the taxation, the incidence would be 2R. 5as. 7p. This burden would be regarded as extremely light in European countries, but the conditions of society in the West and the East are so different that no useful comparison can be drawn.

107. **Expenditure.** There are two ways in which the public expenditure from the revenues of India may be looked at. One is to examine the gross expenditure, just as we have been dealing with the gross revenues of 95 crores for 1894-95. The other is to confine our attention to the net charges. A simple instance will explain the difference. The post-offices and telegraph brought into the treasury 2·6 crores of revenue,

but they cost government 2·4 crores in the same year. The gross receipts and charges were as just stated, but the net result was a gain of twenty lakhs of rupees after deducting all charges for salaries and working expenses. There are four departments of expenditure—namely, post-office, telegraph, railways, and irrigation—in which the State receives back a very large proportion of its expenditure as payment for services rendered. In statements of net expenditure these are called "commercial services."

In the first place, it is well to get a general view of what became of the 95 crores of *gross revenue* received in 1894-95. Of that large sum 71·5 crores were expended upon public defence, public works, and what may be called public faith. Under public defence are included military and marine expenditure, and the cost of police, which together required 29 crores. On public works—namely, railways, works of irrigation, roads, and buildings—a gross expenditure of 32·5 crores was incurred. The public debt involved charges for interest of 5 crores, and pensions, superannuation, and furlough charges took another 5 crores. The post-offices, telegraph, and mint required 2·5 crores. The public health, in the medical and scientific departments, cost 1·5 crores, and education a similar sum. Direct demands on the revenue, in the shape of refunds and assignments, required 1·7 crores, leaving only a little over 16 crores available, of which a half was spent in collecting the land-revenue, the income from opium, salt, customs, and excise, and other taxes. Of the remaining 8 crores one half was spent upon law and justice, 3 crores on general administration and political charges, and the balance upon stationery, printing, and other miscellaneous charges. Looking then at the gross expenditure one can see at a glance that the public debt, the public defence, public works, public justice, and the cost of collection require most of the funds which find their way into the public purse.

But it is generally thought that a clearer view of the expenditure of India is to be gained by deducting the refunds and assignments of revenue, the receipts of the departments, and the cost of cultivating the opium. So calculated, the *net revenue* of the year 1894-95 was 60·6 crores of rupees, and the net expenditure was nearly 60 crores, divided as follows:

Debt services, - - -	4·3	crores.
Military services, - - -	24·2	„
Cost of collecting revenue, -	6·3	„
Commercial services, - -	2·8	„
Civil departments, - - -	13·2	„
Civil works, famine insurance, and other civil service, - -	9·1	„
Total net expenditure, -	59·9	crores.

108. **Home Charges.** Both the gross and the net expenditure mentioned above include charges incurred on account of India in England. These are called home charges, and it would be unnecessary to explain them if there did not exist a strange misunderstanding as to their nature. There is not a factory or a large commercial business in India owned by the natives of India which does not incur similar home charges in the conduct of its affairs. The native states of India, the state of Afghanistan, and every country in Europe find it to their benefit to buy in Great Britain materials

of war, machinery, and other manufactures, for which payment is needed in the coinage of Great Britain at the market rate of exchange. Most of the countries mentioned, all the colonies of the United Kingdom, and a majority of Indian railway or mining companies, have paid agents in London to conduct their business. They also employ the services of British artizans, and many of them are fortunate enough to be able to borrow capital in England upon which they pay annual interest. The home charges of the government of India include stores of all sorts, railway and war material, tools and machinery for public works, agency, furlough, and pension charges, and interest upon the loans raised in London for the public debt or public works of India. To describe the home charges as a "drain" on India is only a correct mode of speech, if the citizen of India, who purchases an English knife or an English book, applies that term to his own expenditure. Just as the British householder purchases Indian tea because it is cheaper and better than Chinese tea, so the citizen and the government of India prudently purchase in England the articles which they require for use in India.

109. **Indian Credit.** There is one infallible sign of a country's ruin or prosperity. To a bankrupt no one in his senses would lend money at any rate of interest, whether he were an individual, a company, or a government. To one on the road to insolvency no one would lend money except at a high rate of interest. But to the British government of India the monied classes of the world are ready to lend crores of rupees, whenever it needs them, at a rate of interest which is denied to most of the nations of Europe; and yet they

know how severe and sudden are the trials through which the finances of India have to pass when exchange falls, when wars arise on the frontier, and when the scourge of famine visits whole provinces. But they also know that the budgets and accounts of the government of India are strictly accurate, and they observe year after year a great investment of the revenues in public works, which cannot fail to make the country richer and afford a perfect security for their advances. In the year which has been chosen in this chapter for an examination of the finances, more than a crore of debt was paid off, and the interest on 92 crores of debt was reduced from 4 to 3½ per cent. No better testimony is needed to the general soundness of the Indian finances, but if further proof were needed, it could be found in a survey of the country and the visible signs of its material improvement to which we must now turn.

CHAPTER XII.

FORCES OF EDUCATION.

110. **A Choice of Benefits.** A few years ago the writer was travelling from Poona to Bombay in the company of three gentlemen at a time when the Great Indian Peninsular railway was breached by floods near Thana. One of the travellers was a Brahman official, the second was a Parsi lawyer, and the third a well-known Mahomedan citizen of Bombay engaged in commerce. A discussion was raised as to the various departments of the British administration, and the question was propounded as to their respective merits. The Brahman gentleman urged that the system of public instruction, and in particular higher education, had conferred more benefits upon India than any other measure of government. The lawyer thought that British justice was a more valuable gift than the university, colleges, and schools. The former laid stress on the coincidence that, when the British government was actually engaged in suppressing the mutiny, it found time and money to establish the first university in India. The latter pointed to the respect shown by the highest

British officials to the majesty of the law. He considered that nothing was at the same time so strange to Indian ideas and so suggestive of justice as the fact that not even the viceroy or the governors would disregard a decree of a High Court, although the court itself had to rely upon the government to give effect to its orders even when they were opposed to the wishes and policy of government. At this point of the conversation the train was shunted, and an engine passed by, drawing a number of trucks full of workmen, tools, and a large crane, as well as sleepers and railway material, in charge of a British engineer. The Mahomedan gentleman jumped up and pointing to the train he said, "There, look at that; the strongest claim which the British have upon the people of India is their power of organization and resource. The break on the line occurred this morning, and now within a few hours an army of native workmen is on its way to repair the disaster under an officer who knows what has to be done and will teach the coolies how to do it. The public works of India are the best school in it."

111. **Educational Agencies.** The total number of children of both sexes under instruction in British India does not amount to 4½ millions, and out of every hundred of children who might be at school eighty-seven never enter that place of education. But it must not be supposed that a man learns nothing except at school. If the State does its duty, its whole administration in every department should be an object-lesson to its citizens. If a government is to draw out (for education means to draw out) the healthy feelings of the people into

sympathy with their neighbours and sympathy with their rulers, it must give them proofs of its sympathy with its citizens. Does the government perform its duty towards me? is a proper question which every subject of the State should ask himself. In previous chapters of this book some attempt has been made to give material for an answer to that question. Does the British government make provision for the public safety? We have seen what it spends upon the army, the marine, and the police of the empire. If space allowed, an account might be added of the formation of fire brigades, of regulations for buildings in crowded streets, and of the wonderful tale of the Gohna landslip and the vast imprisoned lake which, bursting its bonds, rushed down harmlessly into the Ganges, because its dreaded approach was preceded by measures of precaution and telegrams that averted loss of life. Does the government take measures for the public health? The hospitals and dispensaries all over the country, the sanitary departments, the arrangements for vaccination, and the Dufferin fund, enable men and women to answer this question for themselves. Does it let the people starve? Ask the millions who have lately left the famine relief works, the operatives in mills set up by British capital, the labourers in the tea-gardens, and the emigrants to distant colonies, whether endeavours are made in foul and in fair seasons to find employment for the working classes. Is anything done to encourage thrift or assist the raiyats in obtaining loans for their operations? This question touches on difficult subjects, but it is possible to indicate the direction in which material for an answer may be sought. In post-office and other savings banks more than 700,000 depositors hold eleven crores of rupees. It is not an enormous sum, but can any other country in Asia show even a single depositor in a similar institution? The Indian raiyat also knows from experience the value of tuccavee grants advanced by government, and experiments are being made in the Dekhan and in other parts of the country to deal with the difficult subject of indebtedness and exorbitant interest. Every stage, through which the Procedure Code has passed in its several revisions, reminds the public that the government is not indifferent to the subject of thrift and insolvency. The reader can, if he pleases, put to himself other similar questions, but the limits of this book will not permit of further additions to them. It is sufficient to remark that every act or negligence of a government is a lesson to its citizens and therefore an educational force. But for the purposes of this chapter it will be enough to select the following subjects—public justice, public works, postal and telegraphic communications, the press, and schools. The reader will bear in mind that something has already been said about the lessons in self-government taught by municipalities, local boards, port trusts, and cantonment committees, which administer in a single year an income of nine crores of rupees. We may therefore proceed at once to a consideration of the educative influence of the five subjects just enumerated.

112. **Public Justice.** Before the introduction of British rule India possessed no codes of law or procedure, which were equally applicable to all her citizens, whether Hindu, Mahomedan, or of European origin or others. The Indian Penal Code is in itself an education. But although the majority of the

people have fortunately no personal acquaintance with its penalties, there is not a resident in the country who is not aware of the fact that there is a court within easy access which will give him redress against injury or wrong. He knows also that the highest official is not exempt from the obligations and penalties of law, and that there is a gradation of appeals and reviews by impartial judges and magistrates, with whose proceedings, according to law, the executive does not interfere. 2,294,431 suits were before the courts of civil justice in 1895, and in the same year 1,752,360 persons were brought to trial before the criminal courts. Not merely the parties and the persons accused, with their friends, but a host of witnesses, and some assessors were engaged in these judicial or magisterial proceedings, and they could see for themselves the cool and impartial manner in which the trials were conducted. When it is borne in mind that on all sides of the Indian frontiers rough tribal justice provides the only remedy for crime or injustice, the population of India cannot fail to be impressed by their daily experience of the administration of civil and criminal justice in British India, even though the best judges and magistrates are liable to err or are at times misled by false evidence.

113. **Public Works.** The public works constructed by the British government afford a striking lesson in their methods of administration, and in the benefits which the union of India with the United Kingdom has brought with it. No European architect has ever designed a building which surpasses in beauty the Kutab Minar at Delhi, or the Taj at Agra. The ruins of Bijapur, the rock-cut temples of Ellora and

Ajanta, and the palaces of Agra and Delhi, attract to India wondering visitors from England and other distant countries. But not one of these travellers has any doubt as to the relative value of railways, dockyards, canals and bridges, as compared with the noble legacies left by previous rulers in marble and stone.

TAJ AT AGRA.

The public works, built by the British government at the cost of the revenues paid by the taxpayer, make every taxpayer richer by the result. They are what are termed reproductive works. They cheapen the cost of transit, and so enable the people to buy their salt, cloth goods, and other articles at a cheaper rate. They allow the cultivators to send their cotton and other produce to a favourable market, and they add in numerous ways to the comforts and pleasures of life. A lesson too is to be learnt from the cost, as well as the choice, of public buildings. It is not without an object that the most beautiful buildings in the city of Bombay are the University Hall and the High Courts, the two temples of knowledge and justice. There is another point of view from which the public works may be looked at. They are themselves gigantic workshops for the instruction of thousands of skilled artizans and engineers in the construction and adornment of buildings, and the lessons taught to their builders are afterwards applied by them to the improvement of the private dwellings of the people of the country.

Railways perhaps merit the first place in our consideration. It is often said that a government ruling over subjects of various religions and sects cannot alter their social customs and habits of thought, but that railways silently effect a revolution of ideas. At the end of 1896 there were 20,110 miles of railway open to traffic, and 4,282 miles were being constructed, or else sanctioned for commencement. The capital spent on the open lines was 248·6 crores, and from this expenditure the taxpayers receive a very valuable return in the shape of earnings. Some of the railways belong to the government of India, or to native states, and others have been built by companies under a guarantee of a certain rate of interest, or else in consideration of a subsidy. Any one who has travelled by them must have been impressed with the engineering skill applied to them, with the powers of arrangement and foresight required for working them without accidents, and with the regularity and punctuality which they rigidly secure to and demand from passengers. Surely it is not without reason that railways are regarded as a powerful agency in the education of the people.

Irrigation Works deserve separate mention, whether they be canals or tanks. Long before British rule India had discovered the value of tanks and of wells. But canals of the magnitude of those constructed in the last fifty years required a condition of public tranquillity, and a command of science and skill, which India never before possessed. As instances may be mentioned the Upper Ganges canal, which at a cost of three crores of rupees, comprises 440 miles of main canal, and 2,614 miles of distributing channels, supplying water to 759,297 acres: and the Sirhind canal, which cost 3·8 crores of rupees, and consists of 542 miles of main canal, and 4,655 miles of distributing channels. There are 40,000 miles of canal open in India, and more than ten millions of acres are irrigated by them. The outlay of capital upon them has been 37 crores, and the taxpayers receive from them an annual income of 1·5 crores of rupees. The value, however, of irrigation works does not lie so much in their usefulness as a money investment, as it does in the benefits they confer upon the raiyats, especially in seasons when the monsoon fails.

Civil Works are another branch of the public works of India, and there is not a schoolboy in the country who has not seen something of the buildings, and the roads, which government make and maintain out of the public purse. Schools, hospitals, public offices, jails, museums, and courts of law, are constantly rising on all sides of us, whilst our maps show how villages and towns are being joined together by metalled roads, which are not impassable when the monsoon rains descend upon them. Some 4·5 crores of rupees are annually spent by government in providing for these wants, from which the humblest citizens must benefit. If the British government does not spend the taxes upon magnificent works of architecture, like those which adorn Delhi and Bijapur, it at least endeavours to provide a multitude of public works for the practical use and convenience of the masses of the people.

114. **Post-Office and Telegraph.** The extent of India is so large that it will take many years before its postal facilities can be improved to the fullest extent. But enough has been done to make the oldest member of Indian society marvel at this one of the many results of the peace maintained in India by the British government. Was it ever before told in the history of India, that a humble raiyat or petty trader in Lahore could send a letter safely and quickly to Calcutta for the sum of half an anna? The government of India now conveys mails over 122,282 miles, and maintains 30,451 post-offices and letter-boxes. It carries safely 21 crores of rupees a year for the public in the shape of inland money orders. By means of the value payable parcel post it carries 1,878,000 parcels, and recovers from the recipients more than 2 crores of rupees which it pays to the senders. It even remits money in a few hours to the extent of a crore and a half by telegraphic money orders. The postal department sells quinine to the poorer classes, and pays pensions to the pensioners of the native

army. The operations of the post-office are supplemented by a telegraph system of 46,375 miles of line, with 4,046 telegraph offices sending nearly five million messages a year.

POSTMAN.

Can any one, who thinks of this vast network of communications between citizen and citizen, between province and province, and between India and the world beyond it, entertain any doubt as to its influence as a means of education? Something true or false is being diffused through the people by means of the millions of letters and packets carried by post and telegraph. Idle rumours are dissipated by an electric flash, and the first lesson which every nation and every individual must learn for himself is being taught, namely, the lesson not to believe without thought all you hear or all you read. The human faculties of intelligence and discretion are thus kept in exercise, and the waters of village society, which for centuries have run so still, are ruffled by the constant coming and going of the postman. Any one who has heard the jingle of the Dakwallah's bells, waking the silence of the deep forests of Canara, and scaring away by the strange sound the wild beasts of the jungle, must have felt that the postman is a new and powerful influence in the land.

115. **The Press and Literature** are forces of which it is only possible to write in the future tense. There are, it is true, 204 newspapers and periodicals circulating in India, but they are very unequally distributed, and the poet who shall do for modern Hindi or Hindustani what Chaucer did for English, has yet to rise. In countries which have enjoyed for centuries a free press, readers are intolerant of false intelligence or foolish arguments. To an intelligent public, able not only to read but to understand, a well conducted press is essential, and the editors of newspapers in an enlightened country receive salaries which but few of the highest servants of the State enjoy. When India can command for its press the picked men of its colleges and schools, and when the general public take to reading vernacular newspapers with interest and intelligence, the educative

force of its public press will undoubtedly be felt. At present there is in many cases an absence of both of these conditions, and we must look to time and the department of public instruction to gradually supply them.

116. **Department of Education.** A government, which does its best to promote new industries and enlarge the trades and occupations of the people, is not likely to depreciate the value of schools and colleges. If the Indian taxpayer and ratepayer could provide twenty primary schools where there is now one, it would be a source of satisfaction to every one. But for the present the government is obliged to confine its attention to three objects. It provides a small establishment of higher education, which can supply the most pressing wants of the public services and the leading professions; its main object under this head is to establish institutions which shall serve as models to others. In the next place it gives grants-in-aid to all bodies or individuals who are willing to take part in instructing the people and managing schools or colleges. Thirdly, it requires local and municipal bodies to provide, as far as possible out of the rates and a grant from the taxes, for primary education. The operations of the department should be viewed from each of these points of view.

117. **Models of Instruction.** The reader knows well that the scheme of Indian education includes the primary school in which instruction is given in the vernacular; the secondary school, in which English is taught, and the college affiliated to an University, in which education is completed and success rewarded with a degree. The education imparted in secondary

schools and colleges is either technical, or such as falls in with the Arts course of the University. It is desirable to give variety to education, not only because the capacities and tastes of men differ, but also because the wants of society are various, and education ought to fit its pupils to take part in all the services and employments which the country requires. For this reason government provide in their scheme of State institutions, medical and engineering colleges and schools, veterinary and agricultural schools, schools of art and industrial schools. Whenever a new experiment has to be made in the field of education, government lead the way, and especially in the matter of female education and the teaching of science it has been necessary for them to act, because otherwise the attempt would not be made.

118. **Private Enterprise.** But the main object of government is in education the same as we have seen to be the case in trade and famine relief, namely, to get as many persons and bodies as possible to take part in an undertaking which requires the activities and personal interest of a host of fellow-workers. Upon local boards the duty is properly laid of providing for the primary instruction of the children of ratepayers Societies which have the good of the people at heart, and men who adopt the profession of schoolmaster, are welcomed and encouraged in the field of higher education by grants-in-aid. By such means not only are many agents induced to assist, but as a rule they are men or bodies of men, who give to their work their whole heart and time, and produce results which no State agency can by itself ever hope to achieve.

When education was in its infancy in India, the whole burden of showing the way and teaching the people the value of instruction rested upon the State, but as time goes on the funds allotted to public instruction are found to produce better results when judiciously applied to the encouragement of private enterprise and aided institutions. It is a great benefit to give the people schools, but it is a greater advantage to them if they can be led themselves to spread schools and colleges through the land. By maintaining some institutions of all sorts as models, and by offering to willing co-operators an inducement to assist in furthering the cause of education, considerable progress has been achieved in the last half century.

119. **Primary Education.** Private enterprise has not quite the same inducement to undertake primary as it has in the case of secondary and collegiate education. The man who can obtain a degree or a certificate in a technical school has already obtained a possession of some value, which will help to give him the means of livelihood. He is therefore prepared to pay for this result, and self-interest will induce people to open schools and colleges at which they may expect to receive substantial fees. But the classes which never get beyond primary education are poor, and as a rule do not value instruction. If they are to learn to read and write, the State must make it easy for them. It must be expected then that for many years to come public revenue, whether in the shape of rates or taxes, must contribute largely to the cost of primary education. In western countries it is felt that the State owes it to all its citizens to provide primary education for

them, either free of cost or at as cheap a cost as possible. In India the taxpayer is not yet prepared to accept that principle, but it is one which must be kept in view, because no citizen can fully discharge his duties to his neighbours and the State unless he has acquired the power of reading, writing, and reckoning figures.

120. **Statistics.** Only twelve per cent. of those who are of an age to be at school are attending school. There are nearly four million boys at school or college and only 400,000 female scholars. Of the whole number 3,140,000 are in primary schools, and 534,000 in public secondary schools. These results are hardly satisfactory, but they involve a gross expenditure from all sources, namely, taxes, rates, fees, and other funds, of more than 3·5 crores of rupees. All that can be said is that India cannot at present afford to do more, but the need for greater effort and expenditure will be readily admitted by all.

121. **Conclusion.** In the meanwhile the process of education is going on in Indian society amongst millions who have never been inside a school-room or desired to enter one. The action of most of the forces mentioned in this chapter is silent, and it cannot, as in the case of school instruction, be put into statistics; but as long as men have eyes and human faculties, railways, hospitals, post-offices, courts of law, and famine relief camps, besides numerous other incidents of their daily lives, must make an impression on them and add to their experiences and knowledge. It is a great step in public education when the people begin to understand that they are citizens and not slaves, and that, as citizens, they have to play a part in the

administration of their affairs. Some glimmer of this sentiment has fallen upon the millions of the people of India, and to every one who is educated enough to know what citizenship means may be addressed the words: "The position of a citizen of British India is yours by inheritance. It is a great entail. Be mindful of your rights and privileges; be mindful also of your responsibilities. The future will depend largely on your own actions."

> "Are there thunders moaning in the distance?
> Are there spectres moving in the darkness?
> Trust the Hand of Life will lead her people,
> Till the thunders pass, the spectres vanish,
> And the light is victor, and the darkness
> Dawns into the Jubilee of the ages"

GLASGOW: PRINTED AT THE UNIVERSITY PRESS BY ROBERT MACLEHOSE AND CO.

BOOKS RELATING TO INDIA.

BY THE SAME AUTHOR.

THE PROTECTED PRINCES OF INDIA. By WILLIAM LEE-WARNER, C.S.I. 8vo. 10s. 6d.

TIMES.—"An able treatise on one of the most important and complicated problems of our Indian Empire. . . . To students of Anglo-Indian constitutional history his work is of great value."

OBSERVER.—"The book is a monument of industry and of judicial treatment; the whole subject is examined carefully and dispassionately, and every point is emphasised by a wealth of illustrations from Indian history and international law."

A HISTORY OF THE INDIAN MUTINY, and of the Disturbances which accompanied it among the Civil Population. By T. RICE HOLMES. Fifth edition, revised throughout and slightly enlarged. With Four Maps and Six Plans. Extra Crown 8vo.

*** *Adopted by the Civil Service Commissioners as the Text-book on the subject for the Selected Candidates for the Indian Civil Service.*

REMINISCENCES OF THE GREAT MUTINY, 1857-59. By W. FORBES MITCHELL. Crown 8vo. 3s. 6d.

THE RELIEF OF CHITRAL. By Captain G. J. YOUNGHUSBAND, Queen's Own Corps of Guides, author of "Eighteen Hundred Miles on a Burmese Tat," "Frays and Forays," "The Queen's Commission," etc., and Captain FRANK E. YOUNGHUSBAND, C.I.E., Indian Staff Corps (late Political Officer in Chitral). With Map and Illustrations. 8vo. 8s. 6d. net.

FOLK-TALES OF BENGAL. By the Rev. LÁL BEHARI DAY. Crown 8vo. 4s. 6d.

BENGAL PEASANT LIFE. By the Rev. LÁL BEHARI DAY, Chinsurah, Bengal. Crown 8vo. 6s.

A SHORT MANUAL OF THE HISTORY OF INDIA. With an account of India as it is: the soil, climate, and productions; the people, their races, religions, public works, and industries; the civil services, and system of administration. By Sir ROPER LETHBRIDGE, K.C.I.E. With Maps. Crown 8vo. 5s.

MACMILLAN AND CO., LTD., LONDON.

BOOKS RELATING TO INDIA.

A SHORT HISTORY OF INDIA, and of the Frontier States of Afghanistan, Nipal, and Burma. By J. TALBOYS WHEELER, late Assistant-Secretary to the Government of India, Foreign Department, and late Secretary to the Government of British Burma. With Maps and Tables. Crown 8vo. 12s.

INDIA UNDER BRITISH RULE FROM THE FOUNDATION OF THE EAST INDIA COMPANY. By J. TALBOYS WHEELER. 8vo. 12s. 6d.

INDIAN HISTORY, ASIATIC AND EUROPEAN. By J. TALBOYS WHEELER. Pott 8vo. 1s. [*History Primers.*

COLONIES AND DEPENDENCIES. Part I. India. By J. S. COTTON, late Fellow of Queen's College, Oxford. Part II. The Colonies. By E. J. PAYNE, Fellow of University College, Oxford. Crown 8vo. 2s. 6d. [*English Citizen Series.*

BEAST AND MAN IN INDIA. A Popular Sketch of Indian Animals in their Relations with the People. By JOHN LOCKWOOD KIPLING, C.I.E. With Illustrations by the Author. Extra Crown 8vo. 7s. 6d.

ENGLISH MEN OF ACTION. With Portraits. Cr. 8vo. 2s. 6d. each.

CAMPBELL (COLIN). By ARCHIBALD FORBES.

CLIVE. By Colonel Sir CHARLES WILSON.

HASTINGS (WARREN). By Sir A. LYALL.

HAVELOCK (Sir HENRY). By ARCHIBALD FORBES.

LAWRENCE (LORD). By Sir RICHARD TEMPLE.

NAPIER (Sir CHARLES). By Colonel Sir WM. BUTLER.

WELLINGTON. By GEORGE HOOPER.

MACMILLAN AND CO., LTD., LONDON.

www.ingramcontent.com/pod-product-compliance
Lightning Source LLC
Chambersburg PA
CBHW030844270326
41928CB00007B/1216

* 9 7 8 3 3 3 7 3 8 5 6 1 3 *